Guide to
Spiritual
Warfare

Guide to Spiritual Warfare

E. M. Bounds

Whitaker House

Unless otherwise indicated, all Scripture quotations are taken from the *King James Version* (KJV) of the Bible.

Scripture quotations marked (RV) are taken from the *Revised Version* of the Holy Bible.

Editor's note: This book has been edited for the modern reader. Words, expressions, and sentence structure have been updated for clarity and readability.

GUIDE TO SPIRITUAL WARFARE
(formerly titled *Winning the Invisible War*; originally titled *Satan: His Personality, Power and Overthrow*)

ISBN: 0-88368-643-0
Printed in the United States of America
© 1984 by Whitaker House

Whitaker House
30 Hunt Valley Circle
New Kensington, PA 15068

Library of Congress Cataloging-in-Publication Data

Bounds, Edward M. (Edward McKendree), 1835–1913.
 Guide to spiritual warfare / by E.M. Bounds.
    p. cm.
 ISBN 0-88368-643-0 (pbk.)
 1. Devil. 2. Spiritual warfare. I. Title.
 BT981 .B58 2001
 235'.4–dc21

                         00-012127

    2 3 4 5 6 7 8 9 10 11 12 / 08 07 06 05 04 03 02 01

Contents

Foreword*

If you had lived during the early years of the twentieth century, you could have visited a small town and witnessed a most unusual sight. You could have seen Dr. Bounds walking the streets carrying his manuscripts. They would have been written on the backs of old, used envelopes and tied with twine string. He was looking for someone who would undertake to prepare them for publication. Dr. Bounds was continually asking his friends to pray that God would raise up a man who would put his writings into print.

Claudius Lysias Chilton, a scholarly friend of Dr. Bounds, said, "There is no man on earth today except the present editor who would have accepted this mass of matter and devoted the time to give it to the world — a world that will not begin to realize the magnitude and expanse of the work until editor, compiler, and reviewers have been in eternity many ages."

We take this occasion to offer our heartfelt thanks to the friends who have helped to compile, revise, rewrite, and edit the printed and unprinted works of

---

* This foreword is from the first edition of the book, published in 1922.

Dr. Bounds. We thank the Reverend Robert O. Smith of Gainesville, Georgia, for introducing him to us in 1905 and insisting that we needed this apostolic man to teach us to pray and preach the Word.

I here submit a few brief statements from Dr. Bounds' letters to me just before he died. These show his views of Satan before he was taken out of the Enemy's reach forever.

> I am trying to give myself more and more to prayer. Our only hope is in God. I do sympathize with you and pray for you and hold you in loving affection. Rejoice that you are well situated. God save you from your buffeting devil. The Devil is a great help heavenward. The worse agents he has the better we will get on.

> Pray more and more; keep at the 4:00 A.M. hour. God will be for it, the Devil against it. Press on; you can't pray too much; you may pray too little. The Devil will compromise with you to pray as the common standard, on going to bed, and a little prayer in the morning. Hell will be full if we don't do better for God than that. Pray, pray, pray, pray always, rejoice evermore, pray without ceasing, in everything give thanks.

I hope that many souls will be edified and made holier and more devout by the reading of this book. I pray that God will receive additional glory when Bounds' complete works have been given to a needy world.

Homer W. Hodge
Brooklyn, New York

1

Who Is the
Invisible Enemy?

How art thou fallen from heaven, O Lucifer, son
of the morning! how art thou cut down to the
ground, which didst weaken the nations! For thou
hast said in thine heart, I will ascend into heaven,
I will exalt my throne above the stars of God: I
will sit also upon the mount of the congregation,
in the sides of the north: I will ascend above the
heights of the clouds; I will be like the most High.
Yet thou shalt be brought down to hell,
to the sides of the pit.
—Isaiah 14:12–15

The Bible does not give us any direct statements concerning the genesis of the Devil. It gives us no indication of his birth and no description of his creation. The Bible is concerned with the Devil only as he has part in the great crises of man's history. There are only occasional glimpses of him in his work of ruin and death. These glimpses put his acts in striking contrast and opposition to the works and aims of Christ. These inferences indicate an original purity, a high relationship to God, and a heavenly character and conduct. He was and is the head of the angels who left their first estate.

Peter presented the angels' fall as one of the events that illustrate God's justice, its certainty and fearfulness. He said, *"God spared not the angels that sinned, but cast them down to hell, and delivered them into chains of darkness, to be reserved unto judgment"* (2 Peter 2:4). Jude spoke about the same order of God's inflexible wrath when he told us that *"the angels which kept not their first estate, but left their own habitation, he hath reserved in everlasting chains under darkness unto the judgment of the great day"* (Jude 6).

The Revelation of John adds its testimony to this fact:

> *And there was war in heaven: Michael and his angels fought against the dragon; and the dragon fought and his angels, and prevailed not; neither was their place found any more in heaven. And the great dragon was cast out, that old serpent, called the Devil, and Satan, which deceiveth the whole world: he was cast out into the earth, and his angels were cast out with him.*
>
> (Revelation 12:7–9)

Unveiling the Enemy

We can approach the Word of God with the assurance that we will find traces of the Devil's steps and the unfolding of his conduct. God's Word tells us of his evil schemes that have eclipsed so much of earth's brightness and spoiled so much of its promise and hope.

We must have a childlike spirit of trust, and lay aside *"all filthiness and superfluity of naughtiness, and receive with meekness the engrafted word"* (James 1:21). Then we will find satisfaction and illumination of the truth. We will not satisfy our curiosity or find illumination in the fine points of philosophy, but we will find satisfaction and illumination in all things that pertain to the highest truth for the thoughtful, trustful, and prayerful mind.

In the Bible we have the facts and history of man's redemption. Other worlds and other beings are brought into prominence in light of redemption's purposes and plans. These revealed facts, whether incidental or essential, are to our faith what the facts of nature are to the biology student. They must shape theories and settle opinions. They must not be set aside. Reason must not ignore or reject them, but must lay them as the solid foundations of all investigation, the basis of every hypothesis. These Bible facts demand our faith, though we may not be able to reach out into the unknown regions where harmony reigns.

The Word of God brings clearly to light the unseen world: its persons, places, facts, and history. These are revealed not in minute detail, but with enough information to provoke thought and inspire faith.

The Devil Revealed

The Bible does not enter into an argument to prove the being and person of God. It assumes His being and reveals His person and character. Without preface or introduction, the Bible brings God before us in all His majesty and omnipotence. God was at the world's beginning, and He created the beginning of all things. *"In the beginning God created the heaven and the earth"* (Genesis 1:1). How sublime and inspiring is our first glimpse of God! God is revealed not by argument but by work. We learn what He is from what He does.

The revelation of the Devil is the same. He is presented without introduction or ceremony as the Evil One, a graduate of the school of deception and evil. The curtain is drawn, and the chief actor is in full dress. A world is at stake; man is to be seduced; Eden is to be corrupted. No light is shed upon his past history. No knowledge is given of the school where he learned his evil trade. He was before earthly life. Eden does not date his birth. The temptation in the Garden is not the first chapter of his history or the first test of his hellish art.

We have no access to the archives of the past. Eden bounds our horizon, and the Devil is there. Since that time, his history has run parallel with the human race's. Man is the object of his schemes, his destructive devices, and his ambition. Earth is the favorite scene of his exploits. He is at the cradle of every baby, and he has much to do in shaping each person's character and determining his destiny.

The Bible is a revelation, not a philosophy or a poem, not a science. It reveals things and persons as they are, living and acting outside the range of earthly vision or natural discovery.

Biblical revelations are not against reason but above reason. They require the exercise of faith, man's highest faculty. The powers of reason are not able to discover these biblical facts. Yet these facts are for reason's use—its light, strength, and higher elevation. But most essentially, they are to form, nourish, and perfect faith.

The Devil Is a Real Person

The Bible reveals the Devil as a person—not a mere figure, not simply an influence. He is not only a

Who Is the Invisible Enemy?

personification, but also a real person. In the eighth chapter of John, Christ was accusing the Jews for their cruelty, falsehood, deceit, and hypocrisy. Jesus said, *"Ye are of your father the devil, and the lusts of your father ye will do. He was a murderer from the beginning, and abode not in the truth, because there is no truth in him"* (John 8:44).

Many myths have gathered around the person of the Devil throughout the ages. Much poetry, tradition, and even our fears have caricatured his person, exaggerated his character, and colored his conduct. But there is truth in regard to him, naked and simple truth.

There is much truth that needs to be learned about the Devil, and no age needs the plain, unvarnished truth about him more than this generation. We need the light of that truth as a warning, as an incentive to vigilance, and as an inspiration to effort. We need the knowledge about the Enemy—his character, presence, and power—in order to rouse men to action. This knowledge is vital to victory.

Many people deny the existence of Satan and his influence in our lives. Would Christ have used such plain and solemn words repeatedly before His disciples and the Jews to encourage a lying superstition? To deny the reality of demon possession as recorded in the Gospels is simply inconceivable.

The Devil and His Angels

When the Devil fell, others fell with him. This is what God's Word teaches us. We have no record of the number of these fallen spirits. In Ephesians these unseen foes are spoken of as *"spiritual hosts"* (Ephesians 6:12 RV), an uncounted, uncountable number.

How innumerable they are, we cannot tell. The demoniac of Gadara was named *"Legion: because many devils were entered into him"* (Luke 8:30). A legion was somewhat less than six thousand. The total number of fallen spirits must be great, because they were able to permit so many demons to possess one man, or to allow seven to control one woman, as was the case with Mary Magdalene.

There is a statement in Revelation that the *"great red dragon...*[with] *his tail drew the third part of the stars of heaven, and did cast them to the earth"* (Revelation 12:3–4). This may be a reference to the fall of the angels and their number.

The Bible clearly states that the Devil has a host of fallen angelic followers who are ready and eager in their efforts to hurt man and defeat God's kingdom on earth.

2

Identifying the Devil's Personality

Ye are of your father the devil, and the lusts of
your father ye will do. He was a murderer from
the beginning, and abode not in the truth,
because there is no truth in him. When he
speaketh a lie, he speaketh of his own: for he
is a liar, and the father of it.
—John 8:44

The Devil is a personality with definite character. Character can give dignity and value to a
person, or character can degrade a person.
Character is the inner life of a person that forms action and shapes life. Character is a fountain—the head
and stream of conduct.

However, a person's character is often opposed to
his reputation. Character is what we are. Reputation is
what people think we are. The real and the "think so"
are often two different worlds. It would be marvelous if
reputation were based on character, if the real and the
reputed were one. A bad reputation can be coupled

with good character. Conversely, a good reputation can cover up bad character. But the Devil has this characteristic about him: his reputation is based on his character. They are one. The Devil's reputation is bad, because his character is worse.

The Nature of the Devil

The Devil is a created being. He is therefore not self-existent or eternal, but limited and finite. There was a time when he was not, when he began to be. His creation was after the order of the angels. The angels are not the offspring of the family relationship. All the tender emotions, training, sweetness, and growth of infancy are unknown to them. The pains and joys of childbirth are not theirs. Each angel is created, not born. Each is created directly and personally by God. As an angel, the Devil was created good — doubtless, very good. His purity as well as exaltation were sources of congratulation, wonderment, and praise in heaven.

The Devil is a positive character. That is to say, he wears disguises, but his objectives lie in only one direction. He is double faced but never double minded, never undecided, vague, or feeble in his purposes or ends. No irresolution, hesitancy, or aimless action ever spring from him.

The Devil has character if not horns, because character is often harder and sharper than horns. Character is felt. We feel the Devil. He orders and controls things. He is a great manager. He manages bad men and fallen angels. The Devil is an indirect, sinister, low, and worldly manager.

Identifying the Devil's Personality

The Personality of the Devil

Christ is a person, and He puts the Devil in contrast to Himself as a great, mighty, wicked person who is the sower of all evil—as Christ is the sower of all good.

> *The field is the world; the good seed are the children of the kingdom; but the tares are the children of the wicked one; the enemy that sowed them is the devil; the harvest is the end of the world; and the reapers are the angels.* (Matthew 13:38–39)

Is Christ impersonal? Are the children of the kingdom impersonal? Are the children of the Wicked One impersonal? Are not Christ and the children of the kingdom personal and persons? Are not the children of the Wicked One and the Devil himself personal and persons also?

In the Bible the personality of the Devil is established as a reality. He not only is the source of evil to others, but also is the embodiment of evil in a person. The Revised Version makes this clear. The petition in the Lord's prayer, *"Deliver us from evil,"* becomes personal, *"Deliver us from the evil one"* (Matthew 6:13 RV). So we find Christ praying not only that His disciples would be delivered from evil, all evil, impersonal and general, but also *"that thou shouldest keep them from the evil one"* (John 17:15 RV).

The statement by John that *"the whole world lieth in wickedness"* also becomes personal in the Revised Version, where all wickedness concentrates in a person: *"The whole world lieth in the evil one"* (1 John 5:19). Here, too, the Devil is called the *"evil one."* Personality

17

is attributed to him. We saw earlier that fatherhood also is attributed to him, because he is the father of all evil. He is the enemy of Jesus, destructive, active, crafty, cautious, and cowardly.

The Prince of Evil

The Devil and his angels are of a higher order than the fallen sons of Adam, by rank, order, and intelligence. In the Bible the Devil is called a prince, a world ruler, *"prince of this world"* (John 12:31). He is designated as *"the devil and his angels"* (Matthew 25:41). He and they are held accountable for their sins. They are condemned for their revolt in leaving their *"first estate"* (Jude 6), the sphere for which they were created and in which they were originally placed by God.

This fact of their fall, and all the other scriptural statements concerning them, direct and incidental, emphasize that they are persons—living, acting, free, and accountable. That the fallen angels had a chief prince who organized all their movements, who was first in wisdom, leadership, and skill, is clear from all scriptural statements concerning the Devil and his angels.

In 2 Corinthians 11:13–15, Paul said,

> For such are false apostles, deceitful workers, transforming themselves into the apostles of Christ. And no marvel; for Satan himself is transformed into an angel of light. Therefore it is no great thing if his ministers also be transformed as the ministers of righteousness; whose end shall be according to their works.

Identifying the Devil's Personality

The statement *"Satan himself"* is an emphatic declaration of personality. He also has ministers. An influence does not have ministers. Paul was writing about persons who are fraudulent and alluring. He introduced this great leader as the Arch-imposter, the inspirer of all the fraud, hypocrisy, and error of his apostles, who are as false as he is.

In Jude there is a statement that brings into view many personalities:

> Likewise also these filthy dreamers defile the flesh, despise dominion, and speak evil of dignities. Yet Michael the archangel, when contending with the devil he disputed about the body of Moses, durst not bring against him a railing accusation, but said, The Lord rebuke thee.   (Jude 8–9)

The *"filthy dreamers"* were persons. Moses was a great person. Michael, an archangel, is an actual being. What is the Devil, if not a living, active personality?

A High Dignitary

During Moses' time, the Devil was contending with Michael, the highest angelic dignitary. Did the mighty archangel have to appeal for help against a mere influence, a shadowy, dreamy personification? This statement in Jude declares the Devil to be a high dignitary, whose person and presence are not to be treated with dishonor or frivolity.

The following statement in Peter gives further evidence of the fact that the Devil is a person of high nobility.

The Lord knoweth how to deliver the godly out of temptations, and to reserve the unjust unto the day of judgment to be punished: but chiefly them that walk after the flesh in the lust of uncleanness, and despise government. Presumptuous are they, selfwilled, they are not afraid to speak evil of dignities. Whereas angels, which are greater in power and might, bring not railing accusation against them before the Lord. But these, as natural brute beasts, made to be taken and destroyed, speak evil of the things that they understand not; and shall utterly perish in their own corruption. (2 Peter 2:9–12)

Note how James put the mightiest beings in contrast and opposition: *"Submit yourselves therefore to God. Resist the devil, and he will flee from you. Draw nigh to God, and he will draw nigh to you"* (James 4:7–8). Why such a combination and contrast? Is God not a living personality? How can we then reduce the Devil to a mere influence? This passage teaches a personal Devil as surely as it does a personal God.

Why are God and the Devil spoken of in a similar manner in Peter's urgent exhortation?

Humble yourselves therefore under the mighty hand of God, that he may exalt you in due time: casting all your care upon him; for he careth for you. Be sober, be vigilant; because your adversary the devil, as a roaring lion, walketh about, seeking whom he may devour. (1 Peter 5:6–8)

Why cast all care on Him? Why be sober and vigilant? *"Your adversary"* can be no less than an actual being against whom the Christian has to be armed with God's power.

Identifying the Devil's Personality

"Your adversary"! Hate and destruction are his weapons. Can he be less than a person? The Devil is walking about like *"a roaring lion,"* strong, full of passions and deadly hate! Can anything less than a being of fiery passion and infernal power fulfill this divine portrait?

To Peter, the existence and personality of this powerful adversary had had a sad demonstration in his own experience. These words were still on his conscience, heart, and memory: *"Simon, behold, Satan hath desired to have you, that he may sift you as wheat"* (Luke 22:31).

In the Revised Version, another reference to the personality of the Devil may be found in the instructions given in the Sermon on the Mount about swearing, affirmations, and conversation, where Jesus said, *"Let your speech be, Yea, yea; Nay, nay: and whatsoever is more than these is of the evil one"* (Matthew 5:37).

Under the powerful operations of the Cross and the Spirit, as well as the restraining influences of the Gospel, why has evil not been driven from the earth? It is because of the mighty personality and executive ability of the Devil.

Jesus and the Devil

We find many references, hints, and reminders of the power and personality of the Devil evident in the ministry of Christ. By calling him the *Devil*, Christ invested him with an infamous personality and clothed him with all the deceit, craft, and cruelty attached to that name. By using the name *Satan*, Christ put him as the adversary of God and man. By designating him as *"the prince of this world"* (John 12:31), Christ recognized Satan's royal power and ruling authority over evil in this world. The Devil's ability to affect the body with sickness is not merely hinted at but taken for granted in the Gospels.

The conflict between the Devil and Jesus is seen in the Lord's Prayer, that perfect and universal prayer that Jesus puts in the hearts and lips of His people. It contains, according to the Revised Version, this petition of conflict, peril, warning, and safety: *"Deliver us from the evil one"* (Matthew 6:13). Evil is comparatively harmless, feeble, and inert without the presence of its mighty inspirer. Deliverance from the Devil is deliverance from the many evils of which he is the source and inspiration.

Warnings about the Devil

In the sixth chapter of Ephesians, the Christian is presented as a soldier in character, armor, conduct, and courage. Because of the Devil's power, and because the Christian's warfare is mainly against him, we are urged to:

> *Put on the whole armour of God, that ye may be able to stand against the wiles of the devil. For we wrestle not against flesh and blood, but against principalities, against powers, against the rulers of the darkness of this world, against spiritual wickedness in high places.* (Ephesians 6:11–12)

The Christian's comfort as administered by Paul in the sixteenth chapter of Romans is not only the impartation of, *"The grace of our Lord Jesus Christ be with you,"* but also, *"And the God of peace shall br* Satan *under your feet shortly"* (v. 20).

Peter's vital exhortation in his first epistle has a double imperative in it: he not only exhorted the casting of all our care upon God (1 Peter 5:7), but he also gave a loud and urgent call to watch and pray: *"Be sober, be vigilant; because your adversary the devil, as a roaring lion, walketh about, seeking whom he may devour"* (v. 8.)

Moreover, Peter recognized the hand of Satan in the deadly crime of Ananias and Sapphira, saying, *"Ananias, why hath Satan filled thine heart to lie to the Holy Ghost, and to keep back part of the price of the land?"* (Acts 5:3).

The warning that Christ sent to the church at Smyrna to prepare for tribulation recognized the personality and power of the Devil.

> *Fear none of those things which thou shalt suffer: behold, the devil shall cast some of you into prison, that ye may be tried; and ye shall have tribulation ten days: be thou faithful unto death, and I will give thee a crown of life.* (Revelation 2:10)

The explanation of the parable of the tares puts the wickedness, personality, and power of the Devil in contrast with Christ.

> *The field is the world; the good seed are the children of the kingdom; but the tares are the children of the wicked one; the enemy that sowed them is the devil; the harvest is the end of the world; and the reapers are the angels.* (Matthew 13:38–39)

The Devil's Evil Work

The defense of Christ against the Pharisees' charge that He had violated the Sabbath exposes the Devil in his work of evil: *"And ought not this woman, being a daughter of Abraham, whom Satan hath bound, lo, these eighteen years, be loosed from this bond on the sabbath day?"* (Luke 13:16).

The Bible says about Judas, *"And supper being ended, the devil having now put into the heart of Judas Iscariot, Simon's son, to betray him"* (John 13:2). This is a statement not of an influence or a personification, but of a personality outside of Judas, making suggestions to him and urging him on to his act of hypocrisy. This suggestion is strictly in keeping with the character of the Devil.

"And after the sop Satan entered into him. Then said Jesus unto him, That thou doest, do quickly" (John 13:27). This act is greatly advanced in power of action and influence compared to Satan's work in the Garden! There he used a serpent as his instrument. Here he uses a man, a chosen, trusted apostle.

Paul said,

> *Lest I should be exalted above measure through the abundance of the revelations, there was given to me a thorn in the flesh, the messenger of Satan to buffet me, lest I should be exalted above measure.*
>
> (2 Corinthians 12:7)

In this instance, the exalted revelation and experience of the person and power of Christ were closely followed by the revelation and experience of the person and power of the Devil.

Identifying the Devil's Personality

Christ explained the fearful doom that awaits the wicked at the time of judgment: *"Then shall he say also unto them on the left hand, Depart from me, ye cursed, into everlasting fire, prepared for the devil and his angels"* (Matthew 25:41). The final doom of Satan is revealed in these words, *"And the devil that deceived them was cast into the lake of fire and brimstone, where the beast and the false prophet are, and shall be tormented day and night for ever and ever"* (Revelation 20:10).

These extracts are not simply arguments to prove the existence or personality of the Devil. Instead, they are logical, conclusive references to a being whose reality is taken for granted, universally accepted, and thoroughly believed by Christ and the early apostles.

Given this, a singular case would be the person who professed to accept God's Word and yet did not believe in the existence of the Devil. This would be a great breach both in logic and faith. It would be the same as if a person accepted the play *Macbeth* yet failed to recognize the person or existence of Lady Macbeth, whose character forms the plan and nature of the entire plot.

Christ's View of the Devil

Christ's encounters with those who were possessed by devils, or demons, illustrate His constant recognition of these fallen spirits as personal beings. He recognized their distinct individuality. He talked to them and commanded them as persons. They knew Christ, confessed His divinity, bowed to His authority, and obeyed, however unwillingly, His commands.

Jesus made a clear distinction between the human personality who was possessed by a demon, and the personality of the demon who held possession of the person. In His eyes, they were two distinct persons.

The exercising of this distinction gave a severe blow to Satan's kingdom. When the seventy disciples returned and reported about their mission, they said, *"Even the devils are subject unto us through thy name"* (Luke 10:17). Jesus exclaimed, *"I beheld Satan as lightning fall from heaven"* (v. 18), and then, amid their ecstasy and His joy, He renewed their commission:

> *Behold, I give unto you power to tread on serpents and scorpions, and over all the power of the enemy: and nothing shall by any means hurt you. Notwithstanding in this rejoice not, that the spirits are subject unto you; but rather rejoice, because your names are written in heaven.* (Luke 10:19–20)

"Over all the power of the enemy." The Devil is the enemy of Christ and of man. Jesus gave His disciples power over all the Devil's power. To Christ the Devil was a very real person. He recognized his personality, felt and acknowledged his power, abhorred his character, and warred against his kingdom.

3

Recognizing the Prince
of This World

Jesus answered and said, This voice came not
because of me, but for your sakes. Now is the
judgment of this world: now shall the prince of
this world be cast out. And I, if I be lifted up from
the earth, will draw all men unto me.
—John 12:30–32

The Holy Spirit is the substitute, representative,
and successor of Jesus Christ. To the Holy
Spirit was committed the work of breaking the
deadly power of the world by breaking the power of
its prince. Jesus reminded His disciples that the Devil,
who occupied the royal position as the world's prince,
was already judged, condemned, and sentenced.

*Nevertheless I tell you the truth; it is expedient for
you that I go away: for if I go not away, the Comforter will not come unto you; but if I depart, I will
send him unto you. And when he is come, he will
reprove the world of sin, and of righteousness, and of*

*judgment: of sin, because they believe not on me; of
righteousness, because I go to my Father, and ye see
me no more; of judgment, because the prince of this
world is judged.* (John 16:7–11)

Satan may be the prince of this world, but there is
an awful doom awaiting him, because he is the author
of unbelief, sin, and unrighteousness.

What Is Satan's Position?

In these declarations of Jesus Christ, we have the
clear revelation of what the Devil is in his relationship
to the world as a prince and ruler. We understand
why the world is so alien to God, to God's Son, and to
His cause. We understand how attachment to the
world creates estrangement from and bitter enmity
toward God. This happens because the world's beauty
and charms reflect the opposition of the Devil to God.
The world is the sensuous harlot with her snares of
death and hell.

The Devil is recognized by Jesus Christ to be the
prince of this world, not lawfully, but in the world's
rebellion against God. The Devil is not to be submit-
ted to, but to be renounced as a lawless criminal, dethroned as a usurper, and conquered as a rebel. The
Son of God was given this mission: to dethrone and
conquer the Devil.

We see how readily Jesus Christ acknowledged
the position and power of the Devil. When He spoke
of the Devil, He equated him with the world. The
stroke of the Son of God falls on both: *"Now is the
judgment of this world: now shall the prince of this world
be cast out. And I, if I be lifted up from the earth, will draw*

all men unto me." The world is condemned by the power of the Cross.

The Power of the Cross

The sweet, attractive powers of the Cross dissolve the fatal fascinations of the world. The powers of that same Cross cast out the prince of this world from his ruling throne.

Christ affirmed the Devil's high position, but also signed and sealed his destiny and doom. *"God anointed Jesus of Nazareth with the Holy Ghost and with power: who went about doing good, and healing all that were oppressed of the devil; for God was with him"* (Acts 10:38).

Again the Son of God recognized the position that the Devil held as prince crowned by the world's powers. His presence quieted the Son of God. Man's words are not to be victors in this conflict. Jesus used God's words during the Temptation. (See Matthew 4:1–11.) With these He broke the power of Satan's assault and defeated his evil intentions. But Jesus left him still a sovereign with his kingly crown.

The Son of God remained silent at the Devil's approach. The Cross and its deep humiliation and bitter agony, its defeat and despair—it took all these to lift the crown from Satan's brow and bring his throne down to dust and ashes. The adorable Son of God saw *"the travail of his soul"* and was satisfied (Isaiah 53:11).

Jesus saw what it would cost Him and what it would cost every son of heaven to discrown that prince. Because of this, He lapsed into a solemn silence, the prestige of His victory. *"Hereafter I will not talk much with you: for the prince of this world cometh, and hath nothing in me"* (John 14:30).

4

What Is the Devil's Business?

Then was Jesus led up of the Spirit into the wilderness to be tempted of the devil. And when he had fasted forty days and forty nights, he was afterward an hungered. And when the tempter came to him, he said, If thou be the Son of God, command that these stones be made bread. But he answered and said, It is written, Man shall not live by bread alone, but by every word that proceedeth out of the mouth of God. Then the devil taketh him up into the holy city, and setteth him on a pinnacle of the temple, and saith unto him, If thou be the Son of God, cast thyself down: for it is written, He shall give his angels charge concerning thee: and in their hands they shall bear thee up, lest at any time thou dash thy foot against a stone. Jesus said unto him, It is written again, Thou shalt not tempt the Lord thy God. Again, the devil taketh him up into an exceeding high mountain, and showeth him all the

kingdoms of the world, and the glory of them; and
saith unto him, All these things will I give thee, if
thou wilt fall down and worship me. Then saith
Jesus unto him, Get thee hence, Satan: for it is
written, Thou shalt worship the Lord thy God, and
him only shalt thou serve. Then the devil leaveth
him, and, behold, angels came
and ministered unto him.
—Matthew 4:1–11

I f there is any virtue in believing in God, the Devil
may claim this virtue. If there is any praise for always being busy, the Devil may claim this praise,
for he is always very busy. But his character does not
spring from his faith. His faith makes him tremble
(see James 2:19); his character makes him a devil.

The Devil is a very busy character. He does a big
business, a very ugly business, but he does it well,
that is, as well as an ugly business can be done. He
has lots of experience, big brains, a black heart, great
force, tireless energy, and is of great influence and
great character. All his immense resources and powers are used for evil purposes.

Only evil inspires his activities and energies. He
never moves to relieve or bless. He is a stranger to be-
nevolent deeds and compassionate feeling.

Satan's history antedates the history of man. He
and his angels are the only beings who have experi-
enced heaven, earth, and hell. These three places are
familiar to him. He has walked the streets of heaven
side by side with its purest and best. He has felt the
thrill of its purest joys. He also knows the bitterest
anguish of hell and has felt its keenest flames.

What Is the Devil's Business?

The Devil's Big Business

The Devil does a big business on earth. He is a prince and a leader. Men and devils are his agents. The elements of nature are often corrupted by him from their beneficial purposes and forced to destroy. He is busy tempting men to do evil. He has lots of experience in this business and is very adept at it. By his schemes, sin seems to lose its sinfulness, the world is clothed with double charms, and self is given twice the force. He turns faith into fanaticism and love into hate.

A spiritual character can work through other agencies or directly on the human spirit. Satan infuses thoughts and makes suggestions, and he does it so deftly that we do not know their origin. He tempted Eve to take the forbidden fruit. He put it into David's mind to number Israel, thereby provoking the wrath of God. (See 2 Samuel 24.) He influenced Ananias and Sapphira to lie to God. (See Acts 5:1–11.) Peter's yielding to presumption was instigated by Satan. Judas's betrayal was from the same poisonous source. The temptation of Christ was a typical masterpiece of Satan's craft. He tried to dissuade our Lord from God's purposes by showing Him his power to present alternatives with great persuasive logic.

Satan is blasphemous, arrogant, and presumptuous. He slanders God to men and infuses into their minds distorted thoughts about God. He intensifies their hatred and inflames their prejudice against Him. He leads them to deny God's existence and to misrepresent His character, thereby destroying the foundations of faith and all true worship.

Satan does all he can by insinuation and accusation to blacken saintly character and lower God's estimate of the good. He is the vilest of maligners, the most vicious and artful of slanderers. Goodness is the target of his constant attack. He says nothing good about the good, nothing bad about the bad.

Satan is always at church before the preacher is in the pulpit or a member is in the pew. He comes to hinder the sower, to impoverish the soil, or to corrupt the seed. He uses these tactics only when courage and faith are in the pulpit, and zeal and prayer are in the pew; but if dead ritualism or live liberalism are in the pulpit, he does not attend, because they are no danger to him.

Satan's Tools of the Trade

The Devil goes about to do evil and oppress men. Christ expressly declared that some sickness, at least, was directly inflicted by Satan. At every point the Devil is the antagonist of Him who *"went about doing good, and healing all that were oppressed of the devil"* (Acts 10:38). In some way he acquired the power of death and created in men a fearful bondage to it. Through death, Christ works to *"destroy him that had the power of death, that is, the devil"* (Hebrews 2:14).

The Devil put a thorn in Paul's flesh and made a special effort to acquire Peter's loyalty. He directed the whirlwind, kindled the fire, and ordered the disease that devastated Job and his property. He armed the thieving Chaldeans and Sabines against Job, and got control of his wife. He directed the various offices of his empire to ruin this one saint. He will wreck an empire at any time to secure a soul.

Satan sows the tares in the wheat, the bad among the good, bad thoughts among good thoughts. All kinds of evil seed are sown by him in the harvest fields of earth. He is always trying to make the good bad and the bad worse. He filled the mind of Judas, and he inflamed and hurried him on to his infamous purpose. He filled Peter with an arrogant pride that tried to inject human views into the purpose of Christ instead of God's purpose.

The Devil goes about as fierce, as resolute, and as strong as a lion, intent only on destroying. He is restrained by no sentiments that soften and move human or divine hearts. He has no pity and no sympathy. He is great, but he is only great in evil. He has a great intellect, but he is driven and inspired by a vicious and cruel heart.

The Temptation of Christ

At the threshold of Christ's ministry, He was met with temptation by the Devil. The historical account of the situation presents the Devil as a spiritual person. He is the head and embodiment of all evil, making a fierce and protracted assault on the Son of God. We are not informed as to what form he assumed in order to veil the treachery and wickedness of his attack.

The temptation of Christ is noted as one of the preliminary and pivotal facts of His ministry. It cannot be considered a vision any more than can His baptism, the descent of the Spirit, His wilderness trip, or His fasting. It was not an "influence" that tempted Christ. The whole transaction forbids such a conclusion. *"Then was Jesus led up of the Spirit into the wilderness to be tempted of the devil."* The Devil came to Him, and the Devil left Him, and then *"angels came and ministered unto him."*

In this temptation, the methods, hypocrisy, and craft of the Devil may be seen. He comes to the weak, exhausted Son of God with an air of concern. How innocent is Satan's suggestion that Jesus use His power to relieve His hunger! What could be more permissible than to use His spiritual power for physical purposes? How often is this done? Whenever faith is used to serve the natural, the source is always evil.

It is man living for bread alone that makes the temporal become priority. The secular and worldly take on supreme importance. Faith becomes secondary — subservient to money and business. The heavenly is used for the earthly, the spiritual for the natural. We become more intent on daily food than on daily grace, eyeing the seen more than the unseen.

That is the Devil's main business — to materialize religion, to get man to live for bread alone, to make earth bigger than heaven, to make time more intriguing than eternity. What a fearful conflict is being carried on in that quiet wilderness between the fainting Son of God and Satan! It is a struggle between the earthly and the heavenly, between God's religion and the Devil's religion.

The Points of the Conflict

The conflict surges around three points: the fleshly, the presumptuous, and the worldly. This little circle holds all the shapes and forms of temptation — all the crafty devices, all the hidden depths, all the glittering seductions that Satan has devised to swerve men from the allegiance that faith demands.

The Devil's assault on Christ is in striking contrast to his temptation to beguile Eve. It is also in striking contrast to the fearful ordeal through which he tried Job's integrity. Satan cast no suspicion on God's goodness as he did with Eve. He caused no terrific, consuming sorrow as he did in Job's case. Instead, everything was friendly, sympathetic, and inviting.

The second temptation included the fanatical presumption of overheated zeal and brainless devotion. Satan used all the methods of sensational and abnormal religious practices. He tempted Jesus to take the shortcut by which the principles of genuine faith are set aside and superficial substitutes are brought in to make faith more attractive and popular. Presumption seeks to take man-devised methods, which are easy, sentimental, and material, instead of God's lowly way of godly sorrow, strict self-denial, and prayerful surrender.

The last temptation involved the world with its kingdoms and its glory. These are the rewards for devotion to Satan and worship of the Devil—who is the world's god. How the Devil massed all his forces! Religion was invoked. The world and the flesh conspired, under Satan's power, to tempt the Son of God.

The reluctance with which the pure Son of God went into this close conflict with Satan is seen in Mark's statement: *"And immediately the Spirit driveth him into the wilderness"* (Mark 1:12). Nothing can warp this statement into saying that a mere influence tempted Jesus. The temptation of Jesus by the Devil is history—plain, simple, documented fact. Without a doubt or figure of speech, the Bible clearly stamps the whole transaction with personality.

In our text passage from Matthew 4, we read: *"Then was Jesus led up of the Spirit into the wilderness to be tempted of the devil,"* and *"Then the devil leaveth him, and, behold, angels came and ministered unto him."* In Mark 1:13, we read, *"And he was there in the wilderness forty days, tempted of Satan; and was with the wild beasts; and the angels ministered unto him."* These are not figures of speech, but narratives of a transaction and of persons engaged in the transaction. The wilderness and the fasting are literal. The beings are all literal: the wild beasts, the angels, Jesus, and the Devil.

The conflict of Jesus with Satan was not incidental, accidental, or casual, but was essential and vital. Satan held man and man's world in subjection. They had fallen into his hands and were held by him in bondage and ruled by him with desperate power.

The record has been made, *"And when the devil had ended all the temptation, he departed from him for a season"* (Luke 4:13).

The Agony in the Garden

In the Garden of Gethsemane, the season had ended, and Satan was back again as though he had brought seven other spirits more wicked than himself. (See Matthew 12:43–45.) Gethsemane was the sum of the Devil's most maddened and desperate methods. The disguises were off. He appeared there as he really is. It is a rare thing to get a clear, true light on the Devil. He assumes so many roles, acts so many parts, wears so many disguises.

In the Garden of Gethsemane, we see him in life-size form. The air is heavier by his breath; the night is darker by his shadow; the ground is colder, and his chill is on it. Judas is falser still, and Peter is more cowardly, because Satan is there.

What Is the Devil's Business?

On the threshold of Gethsemane, Jesus exclaimed, *"My soul is exceeding sorrowful, even unto death"* (Matthew 26:38), and He *"began to be* [grieved] *and very heavy"* (v. 37). Why? It was because *"this is your hour, and the power of darkness"* (Luke 22:53). Why? *"Now is the judgment of this world: now shall the prince of this world be cast out"* (John 12:31). Everything was silent, and there was an air of dread and horror. Why? *"For the prince of this world cometh, and hath nothing in me"* (John 14:30).

In this situation, the Devil's method with Christ was much different than it was in the wilderness. Then there was an assumed sympathy, the spirit of an inquirer, one anxious to relieve. In the wilderness, Satan offered the most pleasant, attractive, and satisfying ministries to the flesh. There was something of the gentleness of a lamb, the interest and sympathy of a friend. But how that had changed in the Garden! The lamb was transformed into a lion, a roaring lion who was maddened and desperate.

In the wilderness, Jesus could not be seduced by the flesh or self or the world. He must be overwhelmed with dread and horror, thought Satan. His steadfastness must be overcome by weakness and fear. Satan comes to many saints in the fierceness and power of the lion when the gentle inducements fail.

5

Satan's Main Target

[Jesus] saith unto them, But whom say ye that I
am? And Simon Peter answered and said, Thou
art the Christ, the Son of the living God. And
Jesus answered and said unto him, Blessed art
thou, Simon Barjona: for flesh and blood hath not
revealed it unto thee, but my Father which is in
heaven. And I say also unto thee, That thou art
Peter, and upon this rock I will build my church;
and the gates of hell shall not prevail against it.
—Matthew 16:15–18

The Devil is too wise and too lordly in ambition
to confine his aims to the individual. Instead,
he seeks to direct the policies and sway the
governments of nations. In his passion for success, he
goes out *"to deceive the nations which are in the four
quarters of the earth"* (Revelation 20:8).

Satan is an expert in all the arts of deceit. He is an
archangel in execution, and he often succeeds in seducing the nations most loyal to Christ. He leads
them into plans that pervert all scriptural principles.
When the church itself, the bride of Christ, is seduced
from her purity, she degenerates into worldly ritualism.

The *"gates of hell shall not prevail"* against the church. This promise of our Lord stands against every satanic device and assault. But this unchangeable word does not protect the church from the Devil's strategies, which often pervert the aims of the church and postpone the day of its final triumph.

The Perverting of the Church

The Devil is a hydra-headed monster who is multifaceted in plans and wisdom as well as in atrocities. His supreme effort is to gain control of the church, not to destroy its organization, but to pervert its divine purpose. He does this in the most insidious way, so that there is no startling change and nothing to shock or alarm those whom he is trying to undermine.

Sometimes revolutionary and destructive change is introduced under the disguise of a greater zeal for Christ's glory. It is often introduced by someone who is held in high esteem by the local church, but who is totally ignorant of the fact that the measure he is advocating is subversive.

One of Satan's most perverse schemes is to establish a wrong estimate of church strength. If he can create false assessments of local church power; if he can press the material things to the forefront; if he can make these forces powerful in commands and influence, he has accomplished his purpose.

Under the Law of Moses, the subversion of God's purposes and the substitution of material forces were guarded against. The kings of Israel were warned against accumulation of and reliance on material forces. King David was in violation of this law when he yielded to the temptation of Satan to number the people of Israel.

The third temptation of our Lord was intended to subvert the purposes of His kingdom. Satan planned to do this by substituting material elements of strength for spiritual ones.

This is one of the Devil's most insidious and successful methods to deceive, divert, and deprave. He parades the most attractive material results. He praises the power of human planning before church leaders until they are dazzled and ensnared. Then the church becomes thoroughly worldly while boasting of her spirituality. No deceiver is so artful in the diabolical trade of deception as Satan. As an *"angel of light"* (2 Corinthians 11:14), he leads souls to death.

To mistake the true power of the church's strength is to mistake the true character of the church. When its character is changed, then all its efforts and aims are also changed. The strength of the church lies in its devotion to God. All else is incidental and is not the source of its strength. But in worldly, popular language, a local church is called strong when its membership is large, and when it has social position and financial resources. A church is thought to be powerful when ability, learning, and eloquence fill the pulpit, and when the pews are filled by fashion, intelligence, money, and influence. An assumption of this kind is worldly to the fullest extent.

The Source of True Power

The local church that defines its strength in this way is on the highway to apostasy. The strength of that church does not consist in any or all of these things. The faith, holiness, and zeal of the church are the elements of its power. The church's strength does not consist in its numbers and its money, but in the holiness of its members. The church's strength is not found in these worldly attachments or endowments, but in the endowment of the Holy Spirit on its members.

The most deadly symptom that can be seen in a church is the transference of its strength from spiritual to material forces, from the Holy Spirit to the world. The power of God in the church is the measure of its strength. This is the quality God looks for in a church. The power of the Holy Spirit gives the church the ability to accomplish the purposes for which it was designed.

On the contrary, show us a church that is poor, illiterate, obscure, and unknown, but composed of praying people. They may not be men of power, wealth, or influence. Their families may not know one week where they are to get their bread for the next. But with them is *the hiding of* [God's] *power"* (Habakkuk 3:4), and their influence will be felt for eternity. Wherever they go there is a fountain of light, Christ in them is glorified, and His kingdom is advanced. They are His chosen vessels of salvation who reflect His light.

Within the church there are unmistakable signs that she has been blinded and caught by Satan's dazzling glare. The church is being seriously affected by the material progress of the age. We have heard so much about prosperity and gazed on it for so long that spiritual views no longer appeal to us. Everything must take on the rich quality, luxuriant growth, and magnificent appearance of the material, or else it seems beggarly. This is the most perilous condition the church has to face. It happens when the meek and lowly fruits of holiness are discounted by the showy and worldly charms with which material success crowds the church.

We must not yield to the flood. We must not for a moment, not with the hundredth part of an inch, give place to the world. Holiness and devotion to God must be stressed in every way and at every point. The church must be made to see this delusion and snare. This transference of strength from God to the world, this rejection of the Holy Spirit's endowment of might and power, must be recognized as yielding to Satan. The church, more and more, is inclined not only to disregard, but also to despise, the elements of spiritual strength and to set them aside for more impressive, worldly ideas.

The Material Deception

We have been taught to regard the principles of church prosperity as those items that can be seen only in a statistical column. We seek to impress an age geared to the objectivity of secular facts and figures. However, the most vital spiritual conditions and gains cannot be reduced to figures. For this reason, they are left out of the numerical column, and, after a while, they are neither noted nor observed.

If we do not change our methods, our ideas concerning the strength of the local church will become worldly. No matter how imposing our material results may be, or how magnificent and prosperous the secular arm of the church appears, we must go deeper than these for its strength. We must proclaim and reiterate with increased emphasis that the strength of the church does not lie in these things.

These are the gilded delusions that we mistake for the true riches. While we are vainly saying, "[We are] *rich, and increased with goods,*" God has written that we are *"wretched, and miserable, and poor, and blind, and naked"* (Revelation 3:17).

Wealth and prosperity may be the costly spices and splendid decorations that embalm and entomb our spirituality. True strength lies in the godliness of the people. The personal holiness of the members of each church is the only true measure of strength. Any other test offends God, dishonors Christ, grieves the Holy Spirit, and degrades religion.

A church can often make the best showing of material strength when death in its deadliest form is feeding on its vital organs. There is hardly a more damaging delusion than to judge the conditions of a church by its material prosperity or church-related activity. Spiritual barrenness and rottenness in a church are generally hidden by a pleasant exterior and unusual growth. However, a spiritual church converts people from sin soundly, clearly, and fully. Then it puts them on the road to holiness, where they strive to walk in a way that is pleasing to God.

This spirituality is not to be kept in a corner of the church, but is to be its primary and only business. God's church must continue to do this work of converting sinners and perfecting saints in holiness. Whenever this work becomes secondary, or other interests are held to be its equivalent, then the church becomes worldly. When material interests are emphasized, they come into prominence. Then the world comes to the throne and sways the scepter of Satan.

There is no surer way to make the church worldly than to put its material prosperity in the forefront. This is the surest way to put Satan in charge. It is easy for material assessments to become priority by emphasizing them until the opinion is created that these things are most important. When collecting money, building churches, and counting attendance become the evidence of church prosperity, then the world has a strong foothold, and Satan has achieved his purpose.

Creating a Human Institution

Another scheme of Satan is to eliminate from the church all the humble, self-denying ordinances that are offensive to unsanctified tastes and unregenerate hearts. He seeks to reduce the church to a mere human institution—popular, natural, fleshly, and pleasing.

Satan has no scheme that can more thoroughly thwart God's high and holy purposes than transforming His church into a human institution according to man's views. God's right arm is thereby paralyzed, the body of Christ becomes the body of Satan, and light is turned into darkness and life into death.

Men who have religious leadership positions are often blinded by a false attachment to what they think is truth and what they consider honors Christ. They are found trying to eliminate from the teaching of Christ those painful, offensive, unpopular, and self-denying features to which the Gospel owes all its saving beauty and power, and which stamp it as divine.

From the life of Peter we have a painful and most instructive warning:

From that time forth began Jesus to show unto his disciples, how that he must go unto Jerusalem, and suffer many things of the elders and chief priests and scribes, and be killed, and be raised again the third day. Then Peter took him, and began to rebuke him, saying, Be it far from thee, Lord: this shall not be unto thee. But he turned, and said unto Peter, Get thee behind me, Satan: thou art an offence unto me: for thou savourest not the things that be of God, but those that be of men. Then said Jesus unto his disciples, If any man will come after me, let him deny himself, and take up his cross, and follow me. For whosoever will save his life shall lose it: and whosoever will lose his life for my sake shall find it. For what is a man profited, if he shall gain the whole world, and lose his own soul? or what shall a man give in exchange for his soul? For the Son of man shall come in the glory of his Father with his angels; and then he shall reward every man according to his works. (Matthew 16:21–27)

Here is a lesson for all times and for all people. An apostle had become the mouthpiece of Satan! What an alarming, horrible, and revolting picture! An apostle, zealous for his Master's glory, advocated with fire and force a scheme that would forever destroy that glory! The apostle Peter became Satan's agent!

This is the same apostle who had just made the inspired confession, *"Thou art the Christ, the Son of the living God,"* that placed him in highest honor with Christ and the church! Before the words of that divine and marvelous confession had died from his lips, this same apostle became the advocate of plans that would nullify his confession and destroy the eternal foundations of the church.

Satan's Main Target

The Easy Way

Peter, a chief apostle, advocated schemes that would have discrowned Christ of His messiahship and brought heaven's favorite plan to a disastrous and shameful end! What destructive impulse compelled Peter? Satan entered him and, for the time being, achieved his purposes. But Christ reproved Peter, and in the reproof struck a crushing blow at Satan.

"Get thee behind me, Satan" (Matthew 16:23) is a reminder and duplicate of Jesus' response to Satan during the wilderness temptation. *"Thou art an offence [*"stumblingblock," RV] *unto me"* (v. 23), He said. The temptation through Peter was the Devil's trigger to catch Christ in his trap, but Jesus saw through it. *"Thou savourest not the things which be of God, but those that be of men"* (v. 23). The Devil was not in sight. Man appeared, but Satan's views were pressed to the front.

The things that men savor in church planning and church life are against God's plan. The high and holy principles of self-denial, godly living, and surrender to Christ are all against men's view of Christianity. The Devil seeks to destroy the church indirectly. Men's views eliminate all the unpopular principles of the Cross—self-denial, life surrender, and separation from the world. When this is done, the Devil runs the church. Then the church becomes popular, self-satisfying, modern, and progressive. But it is the Devil's church, founded on principles pleasing in every way to flesh and blood.

If this occurs, Christ is no longer in the church. There is no crucifixion of self, no crucifixion of the world, no second coming of Christ, no eternal judgment, no everlasting hell, no eternal heaven. Nothing is left that reminds us of God, because everything reeks of man. Man makes it the Devil's church by turning Christ's church over to human leaders. The world is sought and gained in the Devil's church, but the soul and heaven are lost to eternity.

The very heart of this disgraceful apostasy, this dethroning of Christ and enthroning of the Devil, is to remove the Holy Spirit from His leadership in the church. Satan's plan is to put unspiritual men in leadership to direct the church. Men of great ability and men with the powers of leadership have often displaced God's leadership. The ambition for leadership and the enthronement of human leaders is the doom and seal of apostasy. There is no leadership in God's church except the leadership of the Holy Spirit. The man who has the most of God's Spirit is God's chosen leader. He is zealous for the Spirit's sovereignty, ambitious to be the least, the slave of all.

6

Satan's Subversion of the Church

Jesus answered, Verily, verily, I say unto thee,
Except a man be born of water and of the Spirit,
he cannot enter into the kingdom of God. That
which is born of the flesh is flesh; and that which
is born of the Spirit is spirit. Marvel not that I said
unto thee, Ye must be born again.
—John 3:5–7

Ye worship ye know not what: we know what we
worship: for salvation is of the Jews. But the hour
cometh, and now is, when the true worshippers
shall worship the Father in spirit and in truth: for
the Father seeketh such to worship him. God is a
Spirit: and they that worship him must worship
him in spirit and in truth.
—John 4:22–24

There are two ways of directing the church:
God's way and the Devil's way. God's way and
man's way of running the church are entirely
opposite. Man's wise plans, thoughtful resources, and
easy solutions are Satan's devices. The Cross is retired

and the world comes in. Self-denial is eliminated, and all seems bright, cheerful, and prosperous. Satan's hand is on the controls, and men's schemes prevail. But the church fails under these devices of men, and the bankruptcy is so complete that the court of heaven will not even appoint a successor for the collapsed corporation.

All of God's plans have the mark of the Cross on them, and all His plans have death to self in them. All of God's plans have crucifixion to the world in them. But men's plans either ignore the offense of the Cross or despise it. Men's plans have no profound, stern, or sacrificial denial in them. Their gain is of the world. How many of these destructive elements does the Devil bring into the church, until all the holy aims and heavenly purposes of the church are retired and forgotten?

Society versus Salvation

One of these satanic devices is to pervert the aims of the church. He deludes church leaders into thinking that the main purpose of the church today is not so much to save individuals out of society as to save society, not so much to save souls as to save the bodies of men, not so much to save men out of a community as to save men and manhood in the community. The world, not the individual, is the subject of redemption.

This popular, seductive, and deadly fallacy entirely subverts the very foundation of Christ's church. This trend is so strong that it will sweep away every vestige of the spiritual and eternal. For this reason, we must watch, work, and speak with sleepless vigilance, tireless energy, and fearless boldness. The attitude and open declaration of much of the religious teaching we now hear are in the same strain and spirit that characterized the Unitarian, Jewish, and rationalistic thinking of the nineteenth century.

To save society is a kind of religious fad to which much enterprising church work is committed. Advanced thinkers have elaborated the same idea. They do not realize their true condition, which is one of going backward and not going forward. This backward step entombs religion in the grave where Judaism has been buried all these centuries. It may well be in agreement with the idle dreams of the worldly rabbis to think of regenerating the world and ignoring the individual.

The phrase "to save the world" has a pompous sound. It seems right for the church to apply itself to bettering the temporal surroundings of the individual and improving his sanitary conditions, to lessen the bad smells that greet his nose, to diminish the bacteria in his water, and to put granite in the pavement for him to walk on instead of wood or brick. All this sounds fine and agrees well with a material age. It becomes practical in operation and provides obvious, imposing results. But does this agree with the sublime dignity and essential aim of the church?

Do we need the church to accomplish these purposes? Concerned councilmen, an efficient street commissioner, and the ordinary vigilance of the average policeman will secure these results in the best way. They need no church, no Bible, no Christ, no personal holiness to accomplish these purposes. If the church concentrates its efforts on results that can be better accomplished by other agencies, it will soon be regarded as a nuisance and lose its influence in the world.

A Unique Institution

The purpose of the church of God is far superior to these childish dreams and fruitless philosophies. Its purpose is to regenerate and sanctify the individual, to prepare him by purifying and training him for the high pursuits of eternal life.

The church is like a net cast into the sea. The purpose is not to change the sea but to catch the fish out of the sea. Let the sea roll on its essential nature while the net catches its fishes. What if fishermen spent all their energies trying by some chemical process to change the essential elements of the sea, vainly hoping to improve the stock of fish? They would never catch any fish! If the church used this method, personal holiness would be impossible, and heaven would be stricken from our creed, life, and hope.

To attempt to save the world while ignoring the individual is not only Utopian but also destructive in every way. To save the world sounds like a commendable goal, but it will result in making the church worldly and unfit for her holy and sublime mission. Christ said that gaining the world and saving the man are opposing objectives. (See Matthew 16:26.) Christ taught Peter that his satanic devices would gain the world to and for the church, but would lose the soul. Everything would seem to contribute to the cause of saving the world, when in reality all would be death.

The church is distinctly, preeminently, and absolutely a spiritual institution. It is an institution created, vitalized, possessed, and directed by the Spirit of

God. Her ministers and doctrines have appeal, relevance, and power only when they are channels of the Holy Spirit. It is His indwelling and inspiration that give the church its divine character and accomplish its divine purposes.

The Spiritual Subversion

If the Devil can by any methods shut the Holy Spirit out of the church, he has effectively prevented the church from being God's church on earth. He accomplishes this by retiring from the church the agencies or agents that the Holy Spirit uses. Satan displaces them with natural devices that are rarely if ever the channels used by the Holy Spirit. Christ announced this unchangeable, universal law when He said, *"That which is born of the flesh is flesh; and that which is born of the Spirit is spirit"* (John 3:6).

If a church has a holy preacher, a man of great prayerfulness, of great grace, filled with the Spirit, Satan will use any method to retire him and put in a man who does not pray, but who is eloquent and popular. The church may seem to have gained, but it has "gained" by the substitution of natural forces for spiritual ones, an exchange that has unknowingly revolutionized the church.

A church can be led by holy men who are not highly cultured, but are well-versed in the *"deep things of God"* (1 Corinthians 2:10); who are strong in devotion to Christ and His cause, but not wealthy or of high social position. A church may change these officers and put in men who are in every way decent and moral, but are not noted for prayer and piety. If you put in men of high social position who are capable administrators, the church will scarcely notice the change except for the marked improvement in finances. But an invisible and powerful change will have taken place in the church. It will have changed from a spiritual church to a worldly one. The change from noonday to midnight is not more extreme than that.

At this point, Satan is doing his deadliest and most damning work. It is deadliest and most damning because it is unnoticed, unseen; it produces no shock and excites no alarm.

It is not by the obvious works of evil that Satan perverts the church, but by quiet displacement and unnoticed substitution. The higher is retired, the spiritual gives place to the social, and the divine is eliminated because it is made secondary.

The perversion and subversion of the church are achieved by Satan when the spiritual forces are retired or made subordinate to the natural; when social entertainment, and not edification, becomes the desired goal. This process is intended to soften and modify the distinctly spiritual aims of the church and to broaden what is called the rigid exclusiveness of spiritual narrowness. But in the end it eliminates all that is distinctly spiritual.

That which is in any sense deeply religious will not survive the death of the spiritual. The church's leaders will lose sight of spiritual edification as the purpose of God's church. Instead, entertainment that is pleasing and pleasant will come to the forefront. The social forces not only will retire the spiritual forces, but also will effectually destroy them.

The Modern Church

A modern church with its kitchen and parlor, with its club and gymnasium, and with its ministries to the flesh and to the world is both indicative and alarming. What a contrast there is between the principles that the early church originated and fostered and those that the modern and progressive church presents as substitutes.

The original churches were faithfully spiritual. Their only purpose was to strengthen and cultivate all the elements that combine to make a deep and clear experience of God. They were training schools for spiritual life. They never lingered in the regions of the moral, the aesthetic, and the mental. They fostered no desires or inclinations that were not spiritual and did not minister to the soul's progress.

The early church took it for granted that all who came to them really desired to *"flee from the wrath to come"* (Matthew 3:7) and were sincerely yearning after full redemption. They considered it their obligation to furnish these seekers with the most sacred and exacting assistance. It never occurred to them that entertainment and social gatherings were channels through which God's grace would flow and foster spiritual growth.

These social and fleshly forces are regarded in many denominations as the perfection of spiritual things. These events are arrayed as the mature fruit of spiritual piety, flavored and perfected by its culture and progress. They are ordained as the handmaidens of the prayer and testimony meeting. I object most seriously to the union of the worldly and the spiritual. What have they in common? *"Can two walk together, except they be agreed?"* (Amos 3:3).

What elements of piety are fostered by entertainment and social gatherings? What phases of spiritual life do they promote? What feature of the gymnasium produces faith? Where do you find any elements that are aids to piety? How do social parties produce a more prayerful and holy life? How do they bring the soul nearer to God? How do they form or strengthen the ties of Christian fellowship? Are social clubs not frivolous and worldly? Do parties not cater to and suit the tastes of the carnal and worldly? What unity of purpose and spirit is there between worldly entertainment and witnessing for Christ? The one is intensely spiritual; the other has in it no evidence of spiritual benefit.

We might as well add to the list of heavenly helpers the skating rink, calisthenics, and the gymnasium. If the young people desire to join a club, enjoy a social gathering, or play parlor games, let them do so. But do not deceive them and degrade holiness by calling these things holy institutions that feed the spiritual life.

Creating a Revolution

Disguise it as we may; reason about it as we will; apologize for it as we do; the truth is, we have lost the intensity of our personal spiritual experiences. We have lost the deep conviction about eternal things that is an evident feature of all great spiritual movements.

Many preachers and others have fallen so low in their spiritual experience that they do not cherish these distinct and strongly spiritual methods. Instead, they are devising plans and organizations to gratify their non-spiritual desires, which are midway between Christ and the world. While these desires are not essentially wrong, they do not possess one grain of spiritual power and can never be the channels of heavenly communication.

Satan's Subversion of the Church

It is said that we cannot get church people to attend distinctly spiritual meetings. What is the problem? Are the institutions worn out and no longer of value to the humble, pious soul? Who will dare affirm this? It is said that the desires of the people are low and perverted. Should we then change the methods to suit unsanctified appetites? No, instead, let us tone up their appetites for spiritual things and elevate the tastes of our people.

Let the revolution begin with the preacher. Let him wrestle with God until his ordination vow becomes revitalized so that everyone can feel the pressure of his goal, the intensity of his zeal, the singleness of his purpose, and the holiness of his life. Let the people catch the fire and purpose of his heart until all press on to the regions of perfect love, panting for all the fullness of God. Under this united, divine inspiration, worldly entertainment will be forgotten and become stale. Then the spiritual meetings of the church will become attractive and delightful.

The church cannot become allied with nonspiritual agencies. By doing this, she breaks the tension of her faith and discards the Holy Spirit. She cannot be the supplier of unsanctified desires. Neither is it her business to fall down to the beggarly task of entertaining the people. This is her saddest mistake: when her evening services are surrendered to concerts and lectures; her praise is turned into worldly music; her classrooms become parlors; her social gatherings are more popular than her prayer meetings, and the house of God becomes a house of feasting instead of a house of prayer. The unity of the Spirit and the holy brotherhood are displaced and destroyed to make room for social affinities and worldly attractions.

It is the church's high and royal duty to maintain her spotless fidelity to her Lord, to stress holiness, and to use every means for its advancement and perfection. When this is done, spiritual character and holiness will order all the rest.

7

Overcoming the Enemy of God

I have written unto you, young men, because ye
are strong, and the word of God abideth in you,
and ye have overcome the wicked one. Love not
the world, neither the things that are in the world.
If any man love the world, the love of the Father
is not in him. For all that is in the world, the lust
of the flesh, and the lust of the eyes, and the pride
of life, is not of the Father, but is of the world.
And the world passeth away, and the lust thereof:
but he that doeth the will of God abideth for ever.
—1 John 2:14–17

The world should be renounced by every true
disciple of Christ. To love the world and the
things of the world puts us in open enmity to
God. If we have a relationship of love or friendship to
the world, we are the enemies of God. We need commit no other sin except that of having an attachment
to the world; by that alone, we are the enemies of
God.

61

Christ Jesus said that between the world and His disciples there would be conflict, that the world would hate them. (See John 15:18–19.) Discipleship to both Himself and the world is impossible. The call, the touch, and the choice of Christ, when accepted and obeyed, become the secret and the source of the world's hatred.

Jesus declared the inevitable enmity of the world toward His followers: *"The world hath hated them, because they are not of the world, even as I am not of the world"* (John 17:14). Again, in His High Priestly Prayer, He declared this distinct and eternal separation and conflict: *"They are not of the world, even as I am not of the world."* By virtue of their relationship to Christ, they are separated from and are in conflict with the world.

Spiritual Adultery

This conflict is represented by two persons in the Bible: Adam and Jesus, who is called the Second Adam. Their natures, affinities, and opposition are declared in the clearest language:

> *The first man is of the earth, earthy: the second man is the Lord from heaven. As is the earthy, such are they also that are earthy: and as is the heavenly, such are they also that are heavenly. And as we have borne the image of the earthy, we shall also bear the image of the heavenly.* (1 Corinthians 15:47–49)

Opposition to the world is strongly declared and demanded. The love of the world is hostile to and destructive of the love of God. The two cannot coexist.

Overcoming the Enemy of God

"Ye adulterers and adulteresses, know ye not that the friendship of the world is enmity with God? whosoever therefore will be a friend of the world is the enemy of God" (James 4:4). Nothing is more explicit than this, nothing is more commanding, authoritative, and exacting.

"Love not the world." Nothing is more offensive to God, nothing is more criminal—more abominable—than love for the world. Loving the world violates the most sacred relationship of the soul with God. The purity of spiritual adulterers departs, and shame and illicit intercourse exist. Friendship with the world is heaven's greatest crime and God's greatest enemy.

The world is one of the enemies that must be fought and conquered on the way to heaven.

> *For this is the love of God, that we keep his commandments: and his commandments are not grievous. For whatsoever is born of God overcometh the world: and this is the victory that overcometh the world, even our faith. Who is he that overcometh the world, but he that believeth that Jesus is the Son of God?* (1 John 5:3–5)

The Gospel is represented as a training school in which denying worldly desires is one part of its curriculum.

> *For the grace of God that bringeth salvation hath appeared to all men, teaching us that, denying ungodliness and worldly lusts, we should live soberly, righteously, and godly, in this present world; looking for that blessed hope, and the glorious appearing of the great God and our Saviour Jesus Christ; who gave himself for us, that he might redeem us from all*

iniquity, and purify unto himself a peculiar people, zealous of good works. (Titus 2:11–14)

There is something in the world that makes it a deadly enemy to the salvation of Christ and that poisons us against heaven.

What Is the "World"?

What is this "world" that so effectually alienates us from heaven and puts us in flagrant enmity with God? Why is it that our friendship with the world violates our wedding vow to God? Why is it that love of the world is enmity with God and criminal to the most abominable degree? What are *"the world, the lust of the flesh, and the lust of the eyes, and the pride of life"* (1 John 2:16)?

"The world" includes the mass of humanity that is alienated from God and therefore hostile to the cause of Christ. It involves worldly affairs, earthly things, riches, pleasures, and pursuits that are shallow, frail, and fleeting. These things stir desire, draw us away from God, and are obstacles to the cause of Christ. The divorced or torn relationship between heaven and earth, between God and His creatures, finds its expression in the term *"the world."*

Our English word *desire* expresses the meaning of the word *lust.* It includes the world of active lusts and desires that controls the seat of desire and the natural appetites.

Alford's Commentary says:

> The world was constituted at first in Adam, well pleasing to God and obedient to

Him. It was man's world, and in man it was summed up. In man the world fell into the darkness of selfish pursuits. Man became materialized in spirit and dragged down so as to become worldly and sensual. The world is man's world in his fall from God. "The lust of the flesh" is human nature in opposition to God. The "lust of the eyes" is that sense that takes note of physical things and is inflamed by them. The "pride of life" is the manner of worldly men whereby pride is displayed and pomp is cherished.

Bengel said,

The "lust of the flesh" means those things on which the sense of enjoyment, taste, and touch are fed. The "lust of the eyes" means those things by which the senses of investigation—the eye and sight, hearing, smelling, and feeling—are occupied. The "pride of life" means when anyone assumes too much about himself in words or actions. Even those who do not love arrogance of life may possibly pursue the lust of the eyes. Even those who have overpowered this fault still frequently retain the lust of the flesh. This problem prevails among the poor, the middle class, and the powerful. It is even found among those who appear to exercise self-denial.

John Wesley said,

The "desire of the flesh" means the pleasures of the outward senses, whether of taste, smell, or touch. The "desire of the eye" refers to the pleasures of the imagination, to which the eye is chiefly subservient. It is that internal sense whereby we relish what is grand, new, or beautiful. The "pride of life" means everything that we use to generate respect from other people — fancy clothing, houses, furniture, and manner of living — anything that gratifies our pride and vanity. It therefore directly includes the desire for praise and involves a certain degree of covetousness. All these desires are not from God, but from the prince of this world.

The Enemy of Heaven

This world arrays itself and all its forces against heaven. Worldliness is the epidemic foe of heaven. To live for this world is to lose heaven because of an opposite attraction. The Son of God declares of His disciples, *"Thou gavest me* [them] *out of the world"* (John 17:6), and reiterates the declaration to His Father as one of prime importance, *"They are not of the world, even as I am not of the world"* (v. 16). It remains true to this hour that all the genuine disciples of Jesus are not of the world, but are chosen out of the world, have renounced the world, and are crucified to the world.

What gives the world its fatal charms? What makes its charms so deadly? Sometimes its beauty is all withered, its brightness all night, its hope all despair, its joy the bitterest anguish, and all its prospects decay and desert. But still it holds and binds. We hate to leave it. What is the source of its deadly sorcery and its fatal snares? What is the source of its malignant hate, its hostility to God, and its alienation from heaven?

Overcoming the Enemy of God

This world is the Devil's world. In that fatal hour when man fell from his allegiance and devotion to God, he carried the world with him in his rebellion against God. Man was the world's ruler, and the world fell with its master. This is the reason for its vicious rivalry with and intense opposition to heaven. The Devil has his kingdom here. It is his princedom. He clothes it with all beauty and seductive power as the rival of heaven.

Heaven's trinity of foes are the world, the flesh, and the Devil. The world is first, the most powerful and engaging. All three center in evil, because the Devil inspires and inflames them. The flesh wars against the spirit simply because the Devil inflames its desires. The world gets its deadly and fascinating snares from the Devil. The world is not simply the ally of Satan, but also is his instrument and agent. It represents him with the most servile and complete loyalty.

How to Overcome the World

For a full understanding of the text from 1 John that was already quoted, *"Love not the world, neither the things that are in the world,"* we need to read what precedes it:

> I write unto you, young men, because ye have overcome the wicked one. I write unto you, little children, because ye have known the Father. I have written unto you, fathers, because ye have known him that is from the beginning. I have written unto you, young men, because ye are strong, and the word of God abideth in you, and ye have overcome the wicked one.   (1 John 2:13–14)

67

In order to *"overcome the wicked one,"* the world, its love, and its things must be renounced. At the threshold of many church doors are written these words, which belong to every soul's true betrothal to Christ:

> Dost thou renounce the Devil and all his works, the vain pomp and glory of the world, with all covetous desires of the same, and the carnal desires of the flesh, so that thou wilt not follow or be led by them?

"I renounce them all" was the answer solemnly given, and the preacher, the people, and our own hearts said, "Amen." And let it be amen now and forever. The world must be renounced, and that means renouncing Satan. This is the deadliest blow to his rule.

Friendship with the world violates our marriage vows to heaven. James, in his severe denunciations of the world, made friendship with the world criminal. He declared that to be the friend of the world is to be the enemy of God (James 4:4). We cannot understand this unless we realize he was declaring that the world's friendship is the Devil's religion, *"earthly, sensual, devilish"* (James 3:3). We can get back to God only by renouncing friendship with the world and by cleansing our hearts and hands of its soiling touch. We draw near to God by resisting the Devil. We resist the Devil by renouncing the world.

Counterfeit Religion

The apostle James summed up the distinct characteristics of the Devil's world-counterfeit religion.

Passion, appetite, and pleasure reign and wage war. (See James 4:1–3.) How much of this passion, pleasure, and world religion has there been in the church? Too often its history is a history of passion, strife, ambition, and blood. Its ecumenical councils are the battlefield of passion in its unbridled, most destructive form. Earthly, sensual, and devilish is the divine stigma that marks and mars ecclesiastical history.

Many modern church members and churchgoers are friends of the world; they are its advocates and lovers. They only say prayers in order not to miss praying. There is no drawing near to God, no fighting against the Devil and driving him from the field of action. Their religion, its ceremonies, and its worship descend not from above, but are earthly, natural, and devilish.

"Submit yourselves therefore to God" and *"Resist the devil"* (James 4:7) are the keynotes of unworldly religion. A personal God and a personal Devil are among the primary articles of creed and experience in true religion. Surrender to God, draw near to Him, and live close to Him. Fight against the Devil, and get rid of him by denouncing and rejecting the world.

8

Satan's Mobilizing of the World's Forces

And you hath he quickened, who were dead in
trespasses and sins: wherein in time past ye
walked according to the course of this world,
according to the prince of the power of the air,
the spirit that now worketh in the children of
disobedience: among whom also we all had our
conversation in times past in the lusts of our
flesh, fulfilling the desires of the flesh and of the
mind; and were by nature the children
of wrath, even as others.
—Ephesians 2:1–3

The divine warning against the course of the world, against the fashion of the world, and against the spirit of the world is given because the Devil is directing the world's course. The Devil is creating the world's spirit, and the Devil is cutting the pattern of the world's fashion.

The touch of the world pollutes because Satan's fingers are in its touch. Its desires are deadly and heaven-quenching because Satan kindles its desires.

The world and its things are contraband in Christian warfare because Satan is the ruler of the world and the administrator of its affairs.

In Ephesians, Satan and his legions are called *"world-rulers"*:

> *Put on the whole armour of God, that ye may be able to stand against the wiles of the devil. For our wrestling is not against flesh and blood, but against the principalities, against the powers, against the world-rulers of this darkness, against the spiritual hosts of wickedness in the heavenly places.*
>
> (Ephesians 6:11–12 RV)

The world rulers are principalities and powers that are under the direction of the Devil. They rule this world by ruling the things that rule this world.

The Forces of This World

Satan seizes and directs all the mighty forces of this world! War is seized by Satan, and it is no longer the patriot's struggle for freedom or the defense of home and native land. Instead, it becomes the tool of despotism; it crushes liberty and enslaves freedom. War carries on a campaign of lust, rape, cruelty, desolation, and death.

Money is another of the world's ruling forces that could be used to beautify the earth and to lay up a good foundation against the time to come. It should be used to ease the burdens of the poor, to banish poverty, and to brighten the homes of widows and orphans. Money is a mighty world-ruling power. The Devil rules it, and, instead of flowing at the command of compassionate love, it is diverted by Satan for selfish and unholy purposes. Satan excites men to covetousness and hardens them into callousness. Men become illustrious and esteemed by the world's standards when they are money-getters and money-keepers.

Education is another mighty world-ruling force. Satan chains it, and it becomes the source of pride and ungodly power. Its mighty engineering is turned into "higher criticism." Under the guise of Christian learning, education becomes the most powerful ally to Satan by unsettling faith in God's Word and opening a wide door of skepticism in the temple of God.

In Ephesians 2:2, the Devil is called the *"prince of the power of the air."* The natural forces of the world are under his dangerous control. How many destructive storms and cyclones is he responsible for?

The Flesh and the Mind

And you hath he quickened, who were dead in trespasses and sins: wherein in time past ye walked according to the course of this world, according to the prince of the power of the air, the spirit that now worketh in the children of disobedience: among whom also we all had our conversation in times past in the lusts of our flesh, fulfilling the desires of the flesh and of the mind; and were by nature the children of wrath, even as others. (Ephesians 2:1–3)

In this passage, Paul spoke of himself and the saints. They had formerly lived in Satan's kingdom, and Satan had ruled them by the lusts of the flesh—he had fulfilled *"the desires of the flesh and of the mind."*

We see in these verses how Satan rules throughout the world. He is the *"god of this world"* (2 Corinthians

4:4), and he excites its desires, both low and high—low in the desires of the flesh and high in the desires of the mind. The world fills the passions and chains the mind in its high worldly pursuits and refined tastes. Yet it is all of Satan. The *"lust of the flesh, and the lust of the eyes, and the pride of life"* (1 John 2:16) are of the world, and Satan is the exciter of them: *"Then when lust hath conceived, it bringeth forth sin: and sin, when it is finished, bringeth forth death"* (James 1:15).

> *We know that whosoever is begotten of God sinneth not; but he that was begotten of God keepeth him, and the evil one toucheth him not. We know that we are of God, and the whole world lieth in the evil one.*
>   (1 John 5:18–19 RV)

"The whole world lieth in the evil one" means that the world is in the power of the Devil, is held in subjection by him, and is fixed and established. The Devil is pictured not only as trying to kindle into a flame the desires that may remain in a good man's heart after conversion, but also as enfolding in his arms the whole world and making it subject to his power and submissive to his absolute control.

The Devil's Heaven

The world comes in through many doors, and it comes in many forms. Yet at whatever door and in whatever form it comes, the world is always the Devil's servant. It comes in to do his work as his most obedient and faithful slave. When the world comes in, dressed in its most seductive and beautiful garb, the Devil has fashioned its clothing and ordered its coming.

Satan's Mobilizing of the World's Forces

The world is the Devil's heaven. Its rest, crown, and reward are here. When the world comes in, God's heaven goes out. It fades from the eye and heart. The struggle for it ends, and God's heaven, with its fadeless and eternal glories, is lost.

In these statements from the Bible about the world and the Devil, we see why the world opposes heaven. We realize the enmity between the two. Heaven is Christ's place, the place where He is, and to which He wants men to come. The world is Satan's place. His power is here. To fix our hearts on the world is to be loyal to him. To fix our hearts on heaven is to be loyal to Christ.

Here we have the reason for the world's cruel hatred of Jesus, and why it has so bitterly persecuted His followers. We see why the *"flesh lusteth against the Spirit, and the Spirit against the flesh"* (Galatians 5:17). We see why these are not only contrary to one another, but also at war with one another. The Devil is in the flesh and rules it. Christ is in the Spirit. This world leads away from Christ. It is the invincible foe of Christ.

This great truth is illustrated and enforced by the fact that Christ's work is to get possession of the world and make its power accomplish His purposes. But He establishes a kingdom of heaven that is not of this world. A new power has come in; a new kingdom is established, and a new world made. It will take the fires of the judgment and the new creative power to make a new heaven and a new earth before the stains and ruin of the Devil's death-dealing hands can be removed, and this corrupted, yet beautiful, world can be prepared for God's holy purposes.

The Christian is called to renounce his allegiance to the world. By his very relationship to Jesus Christ, he is lifted out of the world's deadly embraces, and its polluting charms are broken. In this subserviency of the world to the Devil, we have the reason for the world's intense hatred of Jesus Christ. We can see why the world has armed itself with all its forces under the power of the Devil to destroy the cause of Christ. The world's opposition and enmity have always been against true religion, but often its smiles are more fatal than its hate.

9

How Powerful Is the Devil?

Now there was a day when the sons of God came to present themselves before the LORD, and Satan came also among them. And the LORD said unto Satan, Whence comest thou? Then Satan answered the LORD, and said, From going to and fro in the earth, and from walking up and down in it. And the LORD said unto Satan, Hast thou considered my servant Job, that there is none like him in the earth, a perfect and an upright man, one that feareth God, and escheweth evil? Then Satan answered the LORD, and said, Doth Job fear God for nought? Hast not thou made an hedge about him, and about his house, and about all that he hath on every side? thou hast blessed the work of his hands, and his substance is increased in the land. But put forth thine hand now, and touch all that he hath, and he will curse thee to thy face. And the LORD said unto Satan, Behold, all that he hath is in thy power; only upon himself put not forth thine hand.
So Satan went forth from the presence of the LORD.
—Job 1:6–12

We have seen that, instead of minimizing the power of the Devil, Jesus exalted him to the pinnacle of power as the prince of this world. In the significant events of Christ's life, the Devil was the one evil agent whom Christ had in mind and to whose rule He was opposed. We have seen how soon the Devil followed in the wake of our Lord's baptism at the Jordan. Satan came to Jesus after He was anointed by the Holy Spirit and entered into His public ministry.

Power over Satan

When Jesus first commissioned His disciples, one of their assignments was to *"cast out devils"* (Matthew 10:8). Jesus appointed seventy more disciples to go forth to minister, and when they returned to report their work to Christ, they said, with evident surprise and gratification, *"Even the devils are subject unto us through thy name"* (Luke 10:17). He replied, *"I beheld Satan as lightning fall from heaven"* (v. 18). When He was opening His disciples' hearts to receive the great Comforter, He declared that the Holy Spirit was to *"reprove the world…of judgment, because the prince of this world is judged"* (John 16:8, 11).

In one of His impassioned outbreaks, as the pain of His great agony drew nearer, Jesus cried, *"Now is my soul troubled"* (John 12:27). However, the darkness is relieved by a gleam of light in which He sees the ruin of Satan's kingdom and the Devil spoiled, dethroned, and cast out by the power of His cross: *"Now is the judgment of this world: now shall the prince of this world be cast out. And I, if I be lifted up from the earth, will draw all men unto me"* (vv. 31–32).

How Powerful Is the Devil?

Satan's Power over Men

But as the darkness grew deeper and the anguish more bitter, He saw the approaching form of him who controls the powers of darkness. Hushed into silence in the presence of this relentless and cruel Foe, the Son of God said to His sorrowing and awestruck disciples, *"Hereafter I will not talk much with you: for the prince of this world cometh, and hath nothing in me"* (John 14:30).

The Devil's sad and mighty influence is further seen within the circle of the chosen disciples. Peter staggered under the blow of the Devil. The shameful denial by Peter was referred to by Christ before it took place: *"Simon, Simon, behold, Satan hath desired to have you, that he may sift you as wheat: but I have prayed for thee, that thy faith fail not: and when thou art converted, strengthen thy brethren"* (Luke 22:31–32).

Jesus Christ acknowledged the great power and authority that the Devil has in the present deranged order of things. He declared, *"Now is the judgment of this world: now shall the prince of this world be cast out"* (John 12:31).

How defiant Satan is! He opposed Christ stubbornly with reckless and often successful courage. Into the chosen circle of the Twelve he entered, into the one who had been trusted as their treasurer, the receiver and the disburser of their money and their charity.

One of the sacred Twelve was possessed and moved to carry out in the most hypocritical, false way Satan's infamous designs. He came very close to adding Peter to the black list of his disgraceful recruits. It is evident that the Devil had much to do with

Peter's dastardly denial, his lying and blasphemy. The words of Christ make this plain:

> *And the Lord said, Simon, Simon, behold, Satan hath desired to have you, that he may sift you as wheat: but I have prayed for thee, that thy faith fail not: and when thou art converted, strengthen thy brethren. And he said unto him, Lord, I am ready to go with thee, both into prison, and to death. And he said, I tell thee, Peter, the cock shall not crow this day, before that thou shalt thrice deny that thou knowest me.* (Luke 22:31–34)

In the parable of the sower, Christ set forth the unseen but powerful influence that the Devil exerts to neutralize the Word of God. In the record of this parable by Matthew, the Devil is termed the *"wicked one"* (Matthew 13:19). This is a statement of his personality and of the concentration of his preeminent wickedness. He snatches away the seed of the Word with vigilant and diabolical hate. *"Then cometh the devil, and taketh away the word"* (Luke 8:12). He is the destroyer of the seeds of good. Satan is so powerful that the incorruptible and eternal Word of God is prevented from accomplishing its saving efforts because of his vigilance and influence over the mind.

Power to Afflict

In the story of Job and his trials, we see the Sabeans and Chaldeans ready to respond to Satan's suggestion to make their raids on Job's herds. Satan's power is not limited to outside influence, but is direct and powerful, getting on the inside. His suggestions of evil are almost godlike at times. They excite our passions or principles so we cannot see the wrong until it is too late. As we saw earlier, this was true in the case of Satan's suggestion to David to number Israel.

His power is so great that even the best men, who are able to resist his temptations, come under his power for a time. The Christians at Smyrna were so under his power that, while he could not alienate their affections or disturb their loyalty, he could put them in prison. All his life, Paul felt the buffeting inflicted by Satan's power.

When Peter denied Christ, he was in Satan's hands and was on the verge of giving in to his power. Job was for a while put under his power. He was driven and afflicted as if in a cruel tempest in which everything was wrecked and lost except his patience. How great was Satan's power to destroy fortune, family, friends, and reputation!

During the Temptation, the Son of God was led to the pinnacle of the temple and to a high mountain by the fearful spell of Satan.

Angels retired, and heaven hushed its music, was draped in silence, and trembled in awe while Satan's dread power was allowed to expend its dark forces on heaven's Anointed One.

The power of disease was also in the Devil's hands. He smote Job. Christ said of the woman with the spirit of infirmity: *"Ought not this woman, being a daughter of Abraham, whom Satan hath bound, lo, these eighteen years, be loosed from this bond on the sabbath day?"* (Luke 13:16).

Doubtless, much sickness is due to the power of the Devil. To this there is reference in the statements of Christ's work:

When the even was come, they brought unto him many that were possessed with devils: and he cast out the spirits with his word, and healed all that were sick: that it might be fulfilled which was spoken by Esaias [Isaiah] *the prophet, saying, Himself took our infirmities, and bare our sicknesses.*

(Matthew 8:16–17)

God anointed Jesus of Nazareth with the Holy Ghost and with power: who went about doing good, and healing all that were oppressed of the devil; for God was with him. (Acts 10:38)

Power over the Body

Satan's power did not extend to death in Job's case, but he did destroy the lives of his children. Satan was able to hold the Smyrna Christians in prison for only ten days, but thousands of others he held unto death. His own cruel, deadly hands weaved for them the martyr's crown of gold and glory.

The power of the Devil over the body is further seen and illustrated by a number of cases of demonic possession in the New Testament. The Devil had possession of the bodies of some people, using his demons to control them. Some of the people were fearfully tormented in body and almost wrecked in mind. Others had certain functions of their bodies suspended: some were made dumb by him, others were made deaf, and still others were made blind. These cases were many in number and of great variety. Among the most distressing cases were those who were not great sinners. Instead, the young, comparatively innocent ones were the victims of Satan's dread power. The whole person came under the power of this alien spirit. The power of Satan, his nearness and personality, had a constant and destructive manifestation in these cases.

It has been well said that the Gospel narratives are distinctly pledged to the historic truth of these occurrences of demon possession. Either they are true or the Gospels are false. They relate to us words spoken by the Lord Jesus in which the personality and presence of the Devil are distinctly stated. Either our Lord spoke these words or He did not. If He did not, then we must also set aside the concurrent testimony of the seventy disciples. In other words, we establish a principle that will overthrow every fact related in the Gospels.

10

Exposing the Rulers of Darkness

And he showed me Joshua the high priest standing before the angel of the LORD, and Satan standing at his right hand to resist him. And the LORD said unto Satan, The LORD rebuke thee, O Satan; even the LORD that hath chosen Jerusalem rebuke thee: is not this a brand plucked out of the fire? Now Joshua was clothed with filthy garments, and stood before the angel. And he answered and spake unto those that stood before him, saying, Take away the filthy garments from him. And unto him he said, Behold, I have caused thine iniquity to pass from thee, and I will clothe thee with change of raiment.
—Zechariah 3:1–4

The power of Satan is far greater than that of God's highest and earthly saints. In the third chapter of Zechariah, we have the picture of his power with God's high official representatives. Joshua, the high priest, and the angel of the Lord are there. Standing at Joshua's right hand to resist all his righteous acts is Satan. Joshua and the angel realize their insufficiency when contending with Satan, and they send a cry to heaven, *"The LORD rebuke thee."*

Jude also gives us this interesting statement: *"Michael the archangel, when contending with the devil he disputed about the body of Moses, durst not bring against him a railing accusation, but said, The Lord rebuke thee"* (Jude 9).

This obscure text teaches us something regarding this contest between Michael and the Devil. It clearly shows that an archangel's strength is not sufficient to contend single-handedly and alone with the Devil.

The Power of the Unseen

Daniel gives us a glimpse into the power and conflict that exist in the unseen and spiritual world that lies so near our own. This invisible world has much to do with how our spiritual battles are fought and our victories are won. Daniel had been praying for three weeks before the angel and the answer came.

> *Then said he unto me, Fear not, Daniel: for from the first day that thou didst set thine heart to understand, and to chasten thyself before thy God, thy words were heard, and I am come for thy words. But the prince of the kingdom of Persia withstood me one and twenty days: but, lo, Michael, one of the chief princes, came to help me.* (Daniel 10:12–13)

We see how Satan works. If he cannot keep people from praying, he can cause delay in the answer to prayer. In this way he tries to discourage and break down their faith. He wants Christians to minimize the power of urgent, persistent praying.

Exposing the Rulers of Darkness

Satan's invisible influence is seen in his power to use people to cast others into prison. To the little church at Smyrna, Jesus Christ wrote in commendation, warning, and consolation,

> *Fear none of those things which thou shalt suffer: behold, the devil shall cast some of you into prison, that ye may be tried; and ye shall have tribulation ten days: be thou faithful unto death, and I will give thee a crown of life.* (Revelation 2:10)

There are special seats or headquarters of his power, places where the Devil makes his home and rules with an absolute control. Christ referred to this in His letter to the church of Pergamos:

> *I know thy works and where thou dwellest, even where Satan's seat is: and thou holdest fast my name, and hast not denied my faith, even in those days wherein Antipas was my faithful martyr, who was slain among you, where Satan dwelleth.* (Revelation 2:13)

The book of Revelation speaks of some who *"say they are Jews...but are the synagogue of Satan"* (Revelation 2:9). Are there churches that are called Christian, but are really churches of Satan? In Christ's letters in Revelation to the seven churches in Asia, we see how the ascended and enthroned Son of God presented the same view of the Devil. The *"depths of Satan"* (Revelation 2:24) are referred to in the address to Thyatira. In this Revelation of Christ to John, the Devil is still declared to be *"the dragon, that old serpent, which is the Devil, and Satan"* (Revelation 20:2). He is declared to have *"great wrath"* (Revelation 12:12).

Satanic Worship

The Devil's power is greatly and strangely enhanced by his system of worship, which, while it degrades, fascinates many people. The system of pagan worship and devotion is very powerful. It holds its devotees by iron chains. It is not a work of chance, and it does not spring from native religious instincts. It is a system of rare power and skill constructed by a graduate in the craft of seduction and delusion. Satan's hand is at the root of all pagan worship—planning, ordering, and inspiring it. It is this fact that gives it strength and influence.

In the Old Testament, Jeroboam perverted the religious instinct and debased worship for sinister, worldly, and selfish purposes. It is said that he ordained priests for the devils. (See 1 Kings 12:32.) The psalmist declared that the Israelites sacrificed to devils (Psalm 106:37).

The New Testament declares that

> *the things which the Gentiles sacrifice, they sacrifice to devils, and not to God: and I would not that ye should have fellowship with devils. Ye cannot drink the cup of the Lord, and the cup of devils: ye cannot be partakers of the Lord's table, and of the table of devils.* (1 Corinthians 10:20–21)

Again it is declared, *"Now the Spirit speaketh expressly, that in the latter times some shall depart from the faith, giving heed to seducing spirits, and doctrines of devils"* (1 Timothy 4:1).

The intensity and power of the Devil's worship is illustrated in the last book of the New Testament. It shows how his worship will increase in intensity and war against the worship of the Lamb. Almost since the beginning of man, there have been rival altars and rival worship. The Devil is the author, inspirer, and protector of the counterfeit; and Christ is the author, inspirer, and protector of true and pure worship. There are martyrs in the false and devilish, as well as in the true and heavenly. There are also wonders and miracles in both.

Satan's Rank and File

Revelation summarizes the situation:

And they had a king over them, which is the angel of the bottomless pit, whose name in the Hebrew tongue is Abaddon, but in the Greek tongue hath his name Apollyon. One woe is past; and, behold, there come two woes more hereafter.
(Revelation 9:11–12)

These are not lawless *"woes,"* and their authors are not disorderly and reckless mobs. They are organized. Strictest obedience to the Devil prevails. They are *"principalities"* and *"powers"* (Ephesians 6:12) of the first order of creation and of great personal power and dignity. They are ordered and subordered, coordinated and subordinated.

They have the most perfect government—military in its discipline, absolute and orderly in its arrangement. They are under one supreme, dictatorial, powerful head, complete with rank and file and officers. *"For we wrestle not against flesh and blood, but against principalities, against powers, against the rulers of the darkness of this world, against spiritual wickedness in high places"* (Ephesians 6:12).

These high and wicked spirits are everywhere. They fill the air and are intent on evil. They follow the direction of their leader, carrying out his plans with ready obedience and implicit confidence. How loathsome is their nature! How marvelous and miracle-working is their power! How high and kingly is their influence! How military are their purposes!

All this is vividly and strongly set forth in the sixteenth chapter of Revelation:

> *And I saw three unclean spirits like frogs come out of the mouth of the dragon, and out of the mouth of the beast, and out of the mouth of the false prophet. For they are the spirits of devils, working miracles, which go forth unto the kings of the earth and of the whole world, to gather them to the battle of that great day of God Almighty.* (Revelation 16:13–14)

The power of Satan finds its great increase and expression in the efforts and operations of the unregenerate. They are under his power, subjects of his kingdom of darkness. More than that, they are intimate in their connection with Satan; they are so close in unity, purpose, and relationship that they belong to his family. His paternity gives birth and character to them; his fatherhood binds them in a strong embrace.

Satan and the Apostles

How defiant, bold, sacrilegious, and presumptuous is the power of the Devil! He came so near the sacred person of Christ! He invaded the sacred circle of His chosen apostles. Judas fell from his high position—tempted, possessed by Satan, and filled with remorse. He committed suicide, and hell is his for-ever.

Peter acted as the spokesman for the Devil, be-coming the advocate of a non-cross-bearing, non-self-denying worldly religion. He was so affected by the Devil's power that he cursed, swore, and lied. Peter found himself stained and defiled. He was saved only by the prayers of Christ.

John and James fell prey to the Devil when they wanted fire to come down from heaven and burn up the Samaritans. Christ sharply showed that they did not have His Spirit, but the other spirit—the spirit of the destroyer.

Paul had his apostolic plans interfered with and hindered by the Devil. To the Thessalonians, he wrote: *"Wherefore we would have come unto you, even I Paul, once and again; but Satan hindered us"* (1 Thessalonians 2:18). And he bore to his grave the marks on his body of the power of this ancient Foe of apostolic fidelity. (See Galatians 6:17.)

Yet the power of Satan is not supreme. It is lim-ited. This was true in Job's case. Satan could go only so far in afflicting him. And ever since the Son of God came into the world, the Devil's power has been cur-tailed. The Cross gave a shock to Satan and his power. His realm of death has been abolished, and *"life and immortality* [have been brought] *to light through the gospel"* (2 Timothy 1:10). His kingdom received its death stroke on Calvary. The almighty forces of the Gospel are laying hold of the mighty forces of Satan.

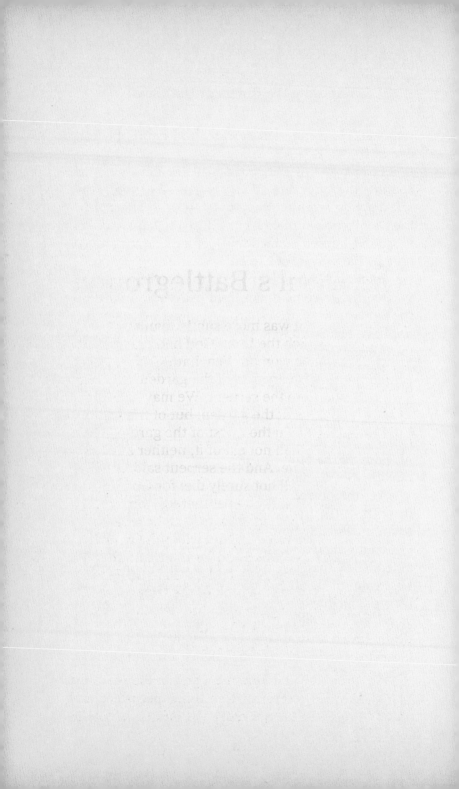

11

The Devil's Battleground

Now the serpent was more subtle than any beast
of the field which the LORD God had made. And
he said unto the woman, Yea, hath God said, Ye
shall not eat of every tree of the garden? And the
woman said unto the serpent, We may eat of the
fruit of the trees of the garden: but of the fruit of
the tree which is in the midst of the garden, God
hath said, Ye shall not eat of it, neither shall ye
touch it, lest ye die. And the serpent said unto the
woman, Ye shall not surely die: for God doth
know that in the day ye eat thereof, then your
eyes shall be opened, and ye shall be as gods,
knowing good and evil. And when the woman
saw that the tree was good for food, and that it
was pleasant to the eyes, and a tree to be desired
to make one wise, she took of the fruit thereof,
and did eat, and gave also unto her husband
with her; and he did eat.
—Genesis 3:1–6

Both in the Old Testament and in the New, the
Devil is represented as being persistent and
tireless in his activities and efforts. In Job, in

answer to God's inquiry, *"Whence comest thou?"* Satan replied, *"From going to and fro in the earth, and from walking up and down in it"* (Job 1:7). This statement reveals his rapid and extensive goings and his repeated and careful observations. He is said to be walking about *"as a roaring lion"* (1 Peter 5:8). Activity, scrutiny, power, and purpose are in his methods.

Thomas à Kempis said,

> Know that the ancient Enemy doth strive by all means to hinder thy desire to be good and to keep thee clear of all religious exercises. Many evil thoughts does he suggest to thee, that so he may cause a weariness and horror in thee, and to call thee back from prayer and holy reading.

The careless and half-hearted Christian knows nothing about the Devil or his devices. But those who serve God are the ones who demand Satan's attention, provoke his anger, and call forth his strategies.

Pastor Blumhart, a marvelous man of faith and power, said, "He who is ignorant of the wiles and artifices of the Enemy, only beats the air, and the Devil is not afraid of him." Blumhart himself is an illustration. "By concerning myself with a person who was possessed," he says, "I became involved in such a fearful conflict with the powers of darkness that it is not possible for me to describe."

Christians may live and die completely unaware of the Devil's existence and hatred. At the same time, Satan is indifferent to their religion because they are not threatening to his kingdom. But a person like Blumhart causes a big commotion and fear in Satan's realm.

The Devil's Battleground

Deceptive Disguises

Satan works by imitation. It is his policy to make something as close to the original as possible and, thereby, to break the force and value of the genuine. This is one of his favorite methods. As Jannes and Jambres withstood Moses by their false tricks, so Satan carries on his work by lying wonders. (See 2 Timothy 3:8.) As his apostles are transformed into angels of light (see 2 Corinthians 11:14–15), so his wonders are looked on as first-class miracles.

What about the revelations of his person? God and Christ have been revealed in bodily shape, by figure, and by representation. Majestic, visible manifestations have been seen by holy men of God. Does the Devil have the power to clothe himself in visible form to the human eye? Can he incarnate himself?

Satan seems to have clothed himself in some visible shape at the temptation of Christ. But the form he used is not recorded. Perhaps he appeared in the form of a man, doubtless a pious man. Or maybe he came as a religious hermit from the seclusion of the desert.

In the days of Christ, Satan revealed himself by taking absolute possession of a person, and he used other personalities through which to manifest his being and power. His manifestations are insidious and deceptive disguises. He sometimes appears as *"an angel of light"* (2 Corinthians 11:14), with the bloom, beauty, and spices of paradise on him. His appearance seems unearthly in splendor, his voice gentle, musical, persuasive, with no traces of the fall.

Physical Attacks

The Devil affects the body and, through the body, affects our loyalty to Christ. Job was tried by his sickness. So the Devil tries us by sickness. In the days of Christ, Satan was very active in affecting the body, not simply by ordinary diseases, but by what is termed *"possessed with a devil."* (See, for example, Matthew 9:32.) In those cases, he worked by breaking down some of the body's chief functions.

His method is to assume any shape that will suit his purposes at the time. Doubtless, there was something in the shape or character of the serpent that gave him easier access to Eve. Dressed as an *"angel of light"* (2 Corinthians 11:14), his appearance commends him to those who are pure and unsuspecting.

As a *"thorn"* (2 Corinthians 12:7), Satan desires to give only pain to those who, like Paul, cannot be seduced or swerved from the fixed course of fidelity. He put the Christians at Smyrna in prison and chained their bodies because he could not shackle their souls. With matchless cunning and unspeakable persistence, he applies his methods to seduce and damn.

The Battleground of the Mind

He has access to the minds of men from which he should forever be barred. But his tricks are so diabolical that he clothes the most sordid act with the fairest guise, and he conceals a world of iniquity with the beautiful colors of the rainbow. He deceived good David and provoked him to number Israel in opposition to God's will, bringing swift and fearful judgment on the nation.

In the parable of the sower, we are taught how the Devil is able to work on the mind and take away any good impressions that are made. *"Those by the way side are they that hear; then cometh the devil, and taketh away the word out of their hearts, lest they should believe and be saved"* (Luke 8:12).

We are also taught how the Devil influences the mind to do the most wicked things, as in the case of Judas. He was chosen as an apostle, into high and holy fellowship, a royal vocation, a select company. Satan had much to do in influencing Judas to the great crime that brought him to despair and suicide.

He readily snatches away from the mind any truth that is superficially received. He also blinds the minds of unbelievers and obstructs the light of saving truth. His processes of taking the Word out of the heart to prevent faith and of blinding the mind to the light of salvation are very common ones with him. He keeps working at it and eats no idle bread. He takes the Word of God out of the unprepared heart and sows tares among the wheat.

He makes people sick for the same reasons he made Job sick. He entices men to do wrong and urges them on to evil.

The Devil goes out into the wilderness and finds us in a fainting, discouraged condition, with our faith weak, the sky cloudy, and our vision obscured. Then he shows us the world from the loftiest peak of observation, clothed in its most attractive form, and tries to ensnare us with its enchanting wonders. He never gets tired of trying to ruin us until the coffin lid is sealed and our happy spirits are bathing in the land where *"the wicked cease from troubling; and…the weary be at rest"* (Job 3:17).

Satan has the wisdom of an archangel and the experience of half an eternity as the captain of all the hosts of hell. He is an expert in the acts and arts of deception and trickery. He has almost inexhaustible resources at his command to serve his purposes. Other than God Himself, a wiser and more powerful spirit than Satan does not live. A more malicious power than he could not exist. There is no greater worker than he. His endless energy and tireless perseverance are the only things in him worthy of imitation. These are the things that make him so powerful and so dreadful.

Yet Satan's *"thorn in the flesh"* (2 Corinthians 12:7) changed Paul's sorrow into joy, his poverty into wealth, his weakness into strength, his reproaches into sweet, heavenly consolations. God must take measures to make Satan's evil deeds work together for good to those who love Him (Romans 8:28).

As an old saint says, "The Devil is but a whetstone to sharpen the faith and patience of the saints." Satan may keep God busy polishing the stones that he makes rough, but the Devil's dirt makes their luster brighter, and they become genuine diamonds of the highest quality.

The Devil's Methods

Satan's methods are as varied as the people with whom he deals. The Devil knows each person's weaknesses and tendency to sin.

To Eve he came in the disguise of a well-wisher, subtle, serpentine, and deadly. He incited her to disobedience by pointing her to greater heights of godlikeness, along paths of sensual enjoyment. A false and selfish accusation was lodged in her mind against God. No danger was apparent, and he used no distressing tactics. Instead, he allured, deceived, and ensnared.

The Devil's Battleground

The method Satan used with Job was much different. He was a man of outstanding character, of whom the Lord said, *"There is none like him in the earth, a perfect and an upright man, one that feareth God and escheweth evil"* (Job 1:8). What methods could Satan devise for the saintliest of the saints?

Satan went to God and accused Job of being selfish in his motives, reducing his piety to the worldly and sinister. No alluring paths, no divergent flowery ways were pointed out to Job by Satan; not a word was said to him. Without a note of warning, tragedy and disaster came as an awful surprise and shock. With one desolating blow, his family of ten children were dead and his princely fortune was gone; one dark hour had robbed him of family and possessions. Stripped naked by the fearful rapidity and depth of his losses, he became homeless, childless, and friendless. His grief was inconsolable and the darkness impenetrable.

The integrity of Job is like a marble column blackened by smoke. He was unshaken by the fiery ordeal, but was still pursued by the Devil. Still Satan insinuated and maligned the genuineness of Job's piety.

He did not recognize Job's noble fidelty or lofty loyalty. Satan continued to attribute low motives as the reason for Job's integrity. With heartless cruelty and malicious lies, he pursued his death-dealing work.

Out of his arsenal of hellish weapons, he came with a loathsome disease. He concentrated on this one saint, adding affliction onto affliction, until his wife was alienated, his friends were estranged, and his enemies were triumphant. There was no relief for his hopeless, bitter grief. His pious reputation has been blackened, his body tortured, his mind put in agony. This is another of Satan's methods: to distress and defame those whom he cannot deceive.

The Deadliest Disguise

To the Son of God in the wilderness, Satan did not come as he came to Job, in frustrating storms of distress, but in the form of apparent sympathy and friendliness. It may have been in the disguise of a saintly hermit in the wilderness. *"If thou be the Son of God"* (Matthew 4:3), he began. (In other words, "You want this matter of Your Sonship to God settled, and so do I. You are very hungry and faint.") He continued, *"Command that these stones be made bread"* (v. 3). This appears to be an innocent and proper way to quickly settle a great question and appease a great hunger.

Then Satan came to Christ and tempted Him with the sanctity of the temple. He gave Him an opportunity to attest His Messiahship before the wondering and awestruck worshippers assembled there. This seemed to be a shorter and better way to give credence to His mission than the slow and thankless process of daily teaching and ministering. It would appear to be easier than marching to the Cross with the dark shadows of its shame and heaviness darkening His way. Finally, Satan's desperate venture was to seduce Christ by the world's array of grandeur, power, and glory.

Satan plunged Job from a serene, cloudless, heavenly height down to a starless and stormy midnight. To the Son of God, Satan would be an available friend to save Him from pain, poverty, hunger, shame, toil, and death.

12

Satan's Clever Strategies

But if our gospel be hid, it is hid to them that are lost: in whom the god of this world hath blinded the minds of them which believe not, lest the light of the glorious gospel of Christ, who is the image of God, should shine unto them....For God, who commanded the light to shine out of darkness, hath shined in our hearts, to give the light of the knowledge of the glory of God in the face of Jesus Christ....We are troubled on every side, yet not distressed; we are perplexed, but not in despair; persecuted, but not forsaken; cast down, but not destroyed.
—2 Corinthians 4:3–4, 6, 8–9

The Devil is seldom seen in his movements and methods. He has the rare ability to get others to do his work and execute his plans.

Blinded Minds

His methods are to blind, to put a veil on the evil results and all the sad consequences of sin. He blinds people so that the evil cannot be seen. Even David, who loved God, was blinded by Satan to the treachery, infamy, and murder in Uriah's case. (See 2 Samuel 11:2–12:10.)

This is how sinners are held in unbelief by Satan. He closes their eyes to all the light and glory of the shining Son of Righteousness. *"In whom the god of this world hath blinded the minds of them which believe not, lest the light of the glorious gospel of Christ, who is the image of God, should shine unto them"* (2 Corinthians 4:4).

The power of the Devil extends to the mind. He can influence the mind, insinuate thoughts, suggest purposes, and excite the imagination. Satan can inflame the passions, stir the appetites, awaken old habits, and fan dead flames or light new ones. He deceived the natural innocence of Eve. He entered into Judas, possessed him fully, and made his half-formed treason complete. Satan was involved in the private council of Ananias and Sapphira, a party to their fraud. He suggested their lying plan to deceive the apostles.

Satan's access to the mind is evident in that he snatches away the divine seed implanted in the soil of the heart, as taught in the parable of the sower. In Corinthians, the Devil is called the *"god of this world."* The Devil uses this world as a veil to shut out the truth of God and the light of His glorious Gospel. He closes the eyes of faith to all the discoveries in the unseen and eternal.

The antagonism between the children of the world who are possessed by Satan and the children of God who are possessed by God is set forth by John:

Ye are of God, little children, and have overcome them: because greater is he that is in you, than he

that is in the world. They are of the world: therefore
speak they of the world, and the world heareth them.
We are of God: he that knoweth God heareth us; he
that is not of God heareth not us. Hereby know we
the spirit of truth, and the spirit of error.

(1 John 4:4–6)

Who is in us? God. Who is in the children of the world? The Devil. Our faith, our hope, and our final triumph are in the truth of the Word of God. *"Greater is he that is in* [us], *than he that is in the world."*

Satan perverts the things that are truly works of God and misemploys miracles to obscure God's glory.

Fear and Discouragement

The Devil often tries to break the soul down and reduce it to despair. In order to discourage us, he tells us that we will never succeed, that the way is too hard and the burden too heavy.

He takes advantage of weak, distracted nerves and suggests fears. Grace is hidden from sight, shortcomings are magnified, and weaknesses are classed as gross sins. Sometimes the fear of death is used by Satan to quench the fire of faith, and the grave becomes something awful.

He darkens the future. Heaven and God are hidden by a thick veil of tomorrow's cares, trials, and needs. The imaginary disasters, failures, and evils of the future are powerful weapons in Satan's hand. He suggests that the Lord is a hard master and that His promises will fail. He works on the corruption that remains in the heart and raises a great storm in the soul.

Samuel Rutherford said,

> Oh, if our faith could ride out against the high and proud waves and winds when our sea seemeth all on fire! Oh, how oft do I let my grips go. I am put to swimming and half sinking. I find the Devil hath the advantage in this battle, for he fighteth in known ground for our corruption. However matters go, it is our happiness to win new grounds daily in Christ's love and to add conquest to conquest until our Lord Jesus and we are so near each other that Satan cannot draw a straw or a thread between us.

Temptations and Feelings

He tempts us to lash out with evil tempers, to speak hasty words, and to be impatient. He tempts us to use carnal reasoning, which is his powerful ally in our minds. We must turn back to Christ. We need more of His Spirit-renewed commitment and thorough self-dedication. By sending prayers upward with uplifted eyes and hearts, we will be able to resist and conquer the great adversary of our souls.

One of the most intelligent and God-honored among the saints wrote, "I have keen inward sufferings, what are termed the buffetings of Satan. Horror at times has taken hold of me. I felt much, but feared more."

The Devil may tempt us to think too little of ourselves as Moses did and too highly of ourselves as Peter did. In one sense, we cannot think too little of ourselves, but in another way we can. Satan persuades us that we are so poor and weak that we can do nothing. And so we are weakened in faith and broken in effort. But Satan's master method is to fill us with self-importance and self-confidence. Then faith is not only weakened but also destroyed. Our efforts and activities may increase in number and vain exhibition, but the seals of self and Satan are on them all.

John Wesley noted:

> I preached on that delicate device of Satan to destroy the whole religion of the heart. Telling Christians not to regard feelings, but to live by naked faith, is, in plain terms, not to regard either love, joy, peace, or any other fruit of the Spirit; not to regard whether they feel them or the reverse; whether their souls be in a heavenly or hellish frame of mind. Satan's method with some is to make them rely too much on feelings. With others he deals the reverse and urges them to discard all feelings.

Naked faith is often nothing but fruitless, unconscious acceptance that brings fruitless, unconscious salvation with it, if it brings salvation at all.

Power over the Enemy

Whatever Satan's methods or clever devices, the words of Jesus, his conqueror, to us are these: *"Behold, I give unto you power to tread on serpents and scorpions, and over all the power of the enemy: and nothing shall by any means hurt you"* (Luke 10:19).

Miss Havergal wrote concerning these verses,

> Why, this is grand—power over all the power of the Enemy. Just where he is strongest

there they shall prevail. Not over the very center of his power, not over his power here and there, nor now and then, but over all his power. And Jesus said, "Is not that enough to go into battle with?"

The Devil's brain is prolific with plans. He has many ways of doing many things. Perhaps he has many ways of doing each thing. With him nothing is stereotyped. He never runs in ruts. Fruitful, diverse, and ever fresh is his way of doing things. Indirect, cunning, and graceful are his plans. He acts by trickery, and always by guile.

According to the Bible, his plans are *"wiles"* (Ephesians 6:11). The original word means to "follow up or investigate by method and settled plan." It is not a bad word, but one of order, arrangement, and methods that are conceived and executed. But when the word gets into the Devil's hand, it is defined by his dictionary. It receives a strong stain, a deep coloring of cunning and trickery.

Sometimes Satan comes to us disrobed of his heavenly garments. He comes as a sharp, pointed, painful, poisoned thorn — a thorn that cannot be extracted by prayer. The saints who have seen most of heaven are often summoned to see most of hell. Saints who have the fullest and most transporting revelation of God often have the saddest experience with Satan.

Paul's thorn meant as much to Paul as his abundance of revelations. His thorn made him more a saint than his vision of the third heavens. Satan only lifted him higher by keeping him lower.

Satan may come to us in his own native character, the thorn-breeder and piercer. He may put thorns in us that no prayer power can extract—thorns that will poison and pain. But the thorn will enrich grace, increase humility, and make weakness strong and glorious. Satan's thorns will clothe necessities with richest attire, and change distresses and persecutions into the most divine pleasures.

Satan's thorns will make room for God's greatest power in us and on us. The Enemy's thorns will make the lowest point of a spiritual depression the highest point of vision. His thorns will make strength out of weakness and wealth out of poverty.

13

Our Most Vulnerable Areas

To whom ye forgive any thing, I forgive also: for if
I forgave any thing, to whom I forgave it, for your
sakes forgave I it in the person of Christ; lest
Satan should get an advantage of us: for we are
not ignorant of his devices.
—2 Corinthians 2:10–11

There are positions and conditions that lie open
to the attacks of Satan. These points must be
guarded by sleepless vigilance. The Devil is a
cruel and mighty foe. To watch him with unsleeping
eye is not only a duty, but also essential to life. Deliverance from hell and the certainty of heaven are involved in overcoming the Devil. Stupidity, neglect,
and being off guard in the conflict with Satan are
much more than mistakes or indiscretions. They are
fatal defeats — eternal and irreparable losses.

The apostle Paul placed his Corinthian brethren
on the winning side in the war with the Devil when
he declared, *"We are not ignorant of his devices."* Ignorance is always an exposed condition. Ignorance is

open to attack and surprise by day and by night. To be ignorant of the existence, character, and ways of the Devil is the prelude to fatal results in the fight for heaven. If this is true, how hopeless is the case of one who not only is ignorant of temptations, but also denies or ignores the existence of the Tempter.

The Devil's great device, his masterpiece of temptation, is to destroy faith in his own existence. God's struggle is to establish faith in His own existence. The Devil's great work is to eradicate knowledge of all spiritual facts, principles, and persons. He who denies or ignores the existence of God, the Devil, good, and evil puts up a fatal barrier to ultimate salvation and paralyzes all efforts in that direction. This ignorance gives one over, chained hand and foot, to the merciless Foe whose existence has been denied and derided.

Nothing advances Satan's work with more skillful hands than to be ignorant of Satan and his ways. To escape his snare, we must have a strong faith in the fact that Satan exists. We must also have an intimate knowledge of him and his plans.

Taking the Devil Lightly

Related to the foregoing vulnerable position is the one that makes light of Satan. Frivolous views of the Devil, his works, or his character, and light talk or jokes that dishonor him are detrimental to any serious views of life's great work and its serious conflicts. Presumption, self-will, and foolishness are the characteristics of those who deal frivolously with these important concerns.

The existence and work of the Devil is a serious matter. It is to be considered and dealt with from the most serious standpoint, and only serious people can deal with it. For this reason, the New Testament gives the repeated note of warning, *"Be sober."* The point is emphatically made in the statement, *"Be sober...because your adversary the devil, as a roaring lion, walketh about, seeking whom he may devour"* (1 Peter 5:8).

Related to this attitude is Jude's incisive and almost rough handling of those who make light of sacred things and sacred persons:

> *Likewise also these filthy dreamers defile the flesh, despise dominion, and speak evil of dignities. Yet Michael the archangel, when contending with the devil he disputed about the body of Moses, durst not bring against him a railing accusation, but said, The Lord rebuke thee. But these speak evil of those things which they know not: but what they know naturally, as brute beasts, in those things they corrupt themselves.* (Jude 8–10)

Peter also had something to say about this same class of flippant, irreverent talkers:

> *Presumptuous are they, selfwilled, they are not afraid to speak evil of dignities. Whereas angels, which are greater in power and might, bring not railing accusation against them before the Lord. But these, as natural brute beasts, made to be taken and destroyed, speak evil of the things that they understand not; and shall utterly perish in their own corruption; and shall receive the reward of unrighteous-ness, as they that count it pleasure to riot in the day time. Spots they are and blemishes, sporting themselves with their own deceivings while they feast with you.* (2 Peter 2:10–13)

A paralyzing attitude in which we remain to listen to Satan's insinuations is fatal. This was Eve's mistake. His tongue is smooth as oil; his words circulate and inflame like poison. For this reason, our position must be one of bristling opposition, fortified for war, with no barriers down, no open gates, no low places. Fenced in and barricaded against the Devil is the only safe place.

An Unforgiving Spirit

An unforgiving spirit invites satanic possession. His favorite realm is the spirit. To corrupt our spirits, to provoke us to retaliation, revenge, or unmercifulness—that is his chosen work and his most common and successful device. Paul brought this device out into the open so that we can thwart Satan's plans.

> *To whom ye forgive any thing, I forgive also: for if I forgave any thing, to whom I forgave it, for your sakes forgave I it in the person of Christ; lest Satan should get an advantage of us: for we are not ignorant of his devices.* (2 Corinthians 2:10–11)

When Satan generates an unforgiving spirit in us, then he has us, and we are on his ground. Then wicked men and good men, all kinds of people, are likely to do us harm, sometimes at vital and very sensitive points. Sometimes they unconsciously wrong us and sometimes they do it knowingly and willfully. As soon as a spirit of unkindness possesses us for the wrong done to us, Satan has the upper hand.

Oaths and Swearing

Let me quote the warning words of our Savior:

Our Most Vulnerable Areas

*Again, ye have heard that it was said to them of old
time, Thou shalt not forswear thyself, but shalt per-
form unto the Lord thine oaths: but I say unto you,
Swear not at all; neither by the heaven, for it is the
throne of God; nor by the earth, for it is the footstool
of his feet; nor by Jerusalem, for it is the city of the
great King. Neither shalt thou swear by thy head,
for thou canst not make one hair white or black. But
let your speech be, Yea, yea; Nay, nay: and whatsoever is more than these is of the evil one.*

(Matthew 5:33–37 RV)

The injunction is against using strong oaths in
language. Expletives and appeals added to our words
are wrong and expose us to the snare of Satan. *"In the
multitude of words,"* says Proverbs, *"there wanteth not
sin"* (Proverbs 10:19).

Satan tempts us to use assertions and declarations
to confirm the truth of what we are saying. When we
use additional words as a way of substantiating the
truth of those already spoken, they expose us to Satan's power. *"But above all things, my brethren, swear
not, neither by heaven, neither by the earth, neither by any
other oath: but let your yea be yea; and your nay, nay; lest
ye fall into condemnation"* (James 5:12). James sealed
the words of Christ. The Devil lies concealed in many
words. Simplicity, brevity, and seriousness of words
will mightily hinder and thwart his ensnaring plans.

It is so easy for the Devil to stop us just short of a
faith that will save, because of this type of wordiness.
There are many speeches, prefaces, and introductions
that are sometimes quite monotonous. They are often
headed in the right direction, but they do not bring us
to the heart of the matter. Like Sarah, they start with

the full intent to go to Canaan, but stop at Haran and dwell there. (See Genesis 11:31.) Like Jacob, Shechem slows their steps and holds them instead of Bethel. (See Genesis 35:1–6.)

Religious Fanaticism

Dangerous excessiveness takes other forms, as well. There are those who are earnestly striving after that *"holiness, without which no man shall see the Lord"* (Hebrews 12:14), but Satan tempts them to go a little too far, and their zeal degenerates into ungodly fervor that causes division in the church.

Strengths are turned into weaknesses: Strict earnestness degenerates into severity, gentleness into weakness. Energetic activity turns into imprudent meddling and narrowness. Calm moderation soon becomes careless acquiesence. Bold convictions become intolerant, opinionated, and bigoted. Respect for the convictions of others degenerates into paralyzing indifference and skeptical laziness. Eager trust lapses into presumption and haughtiness. Cautious wisdom soon becomes cowardice and hesitating anxiety. Confession and profession evaporate into dry religious duty.

Satan watches and is always alert to try to hold us back from the final goal. Or he works in the opposite way to drive us on with an impetuous and obsessed spirit to go beyond the goal. It is Satan's purpose to uncover our strongest positions and turn them into vulnerable areas.

Being Unequally Yoked

Becoming unequally yoked with unbelievers in intimate and confiding friendships creates exposed positions of which the Devil takes great advantage. Partnership in business or the more sacred union of marriage with unbelievers is perilous to the believer in Jesus Christ.

> *Be ye not unequally yoked together with unbelievers: for what fellowship hath righteousness with unrighteousness? and what communion hath light with darkness? And what concord hath Christ with Belial? or what part hath he that believeth with an infidel?*
> (2 Corinthians 6:14–15)

Satan is called *"Belial,"* which means someone who is worthless, contemptible, and wicked. He and Christ cannot be joined in agreement. No unequal yoking, no fellowship, no communion, no agreement can exist. The result is contamination and impurity. The fruit of these voluntary close yokings is a weakened spiritual condition. Under the law, an ox and an ass could not be yoked together. Under the Spirit, Christ and Satan can have no agreements.

Separation, cleansing, and perfected holiness are necessary to secure the vantage ground against Satan. The Bible gives strong, explicit, and comprehensive commands against union, communion, or intimate association with unbelievers. For those unequally yoked there can be no pulling together, no fellowship, no sharing, no communion, no intimacy, no agreement, no voting together.

Commentators have found in the above verses from 2 Corinthians, Paul's fine command of the Greek language. We find in them the fire of fervent and profound convictions. They demand self-denying abstinence from forming intimate and voluntary associations with the unbelieving world in business, pleasure, or social pursuits.

Paul laid down this rule in his first epistle to the Corinthians:

> *I wrote unto you in an epistle not to company with fornicators: yet not altogether with the fornicators of this world, or with the covetous, or extortioners, or with idolaters; for then must ye needs go out of the world. But now I have written unto you not to keep company, if any man that is called a brother be a fornicator, or covetous, or an idolater, or a railer, or a drunkard, or an extortioner; with such an one no not to eat.* (1 Corinthians 5:9–11)

Paul is not objecting to casual, courteous Christian conversation but to more intimate and lasting relationships.

Worldly Friendships

James defined and opposed these worldly relationships and attachments as vulnerable positions that result in the most criminal violation of the holiest relationship. *"Ye adulterers and adulteresses, know ye not that the friendship of the world is enmity with God? whosoever therefore will be a friend of the world is the enemy of God"* (James 4:4). By such associations, the marriage vow of God is broken.

Dean Alford, commenting on this passage, said,

> Of the world, it means men and men's interest, ambitions and employments, insofar as they are without God. The man who is taken

Our Most Vulnerable Areas

out of the world by Christ cannot again become the friend and companion of worldly men and their schemes, without passing into enmity with God. God and the world stand opposed to one another, so that a man cannot join the one without deserting the other. He, therefore, who desires to be the friend of the world, and sets his mind and thought and wish that way, must make up his mind to be God's enemy.

We may ask, "But shouldn't I be friendly with my relatives, whether they fear God or not?" There is nothing we can do to change our family relationships, but there are some that are nearer to us than others. The nearest relatives are husbands and wives. They have taken each other for better or worse, and they must make the best of each other. God has joined them together, and no one can put them asunder.

Parents are also very closely connected with their children. You cannot part with your children while they are young, because it is your duty to "train them up in the way wherein they should go." (See Proverbs 22:6.) Once they are grown, your relationship with them changes, and you must use your own discretion to determine how close you will be to them.

Children must also determine how long it is expedient for them to remain with their parents. In general, if their parents do not fear God, they should leave them as soon as is convenient.

As for all other relatives, even brothers or sisters, if they are of the world, you are under no obligation to be closely associated with them. You may be courteous and friendly, but at a distance.

GUIDE TO SPIRITUAL WARFARE

The Only Escape

Since *"friendship of the world is enmity with God"*
(James 4:4), the only way to heaven is to avoid all intimacy with worldly people. Whatever the cost, flee
spiritual adultery! Have no friendship with the world.
No matter how tempted you are by profit or pleasure,
do not become intimate with worldly-minded people.
And if you are already involved with anyone who is
of the world, break off the relationship without delay.

Your life is at stake—eternal life or eternal death.
Is it not better to go into life having one eye or one
hand, than having both, to be cast into hellfire? (See
Matthew 5:29–30.) No matter how tempted you are to
continue, have no friendship with the world. Look
around and see the dreadful effects it has produced
among your brethren! How many of the mighty have
fallen because of this very thing! They would heed no
warning. They conversed intimately with worldly-
minded people until they themselves were back in the
world again.

Oh, *"come out from among them"*! (2 Corinthians
6:17). Come out from all unholy men, however harmless they may appear, *"and be ye separate"* (v. 17)—at
least have no intimacy with them. Your *"fellowship is
with the Father, and with his Son Jesus Christ"* (1 John
1:3). So let your fellowship be with those, and those
only, who at least seek the Lord Jesus Christ in sin-
cerity. Then *"ye shall be,"* in a special sense, *"my sons
and daughters, saith the Lord Almighty"* (2 Corinthians
6:18).

How Satan surrounds us! How strongly he holds
us! How he entangles, chains, and binds us with
worldly associations! We lie in the sweet friendship,

118

the embraces, and the counsel of these worldly ones, while they lie in the arms of the Wicked One.

A Simple Answer

If simplicity is removed from our faith, our defenses against Satan are weakened.

> *I am jealous over you with godly jealousy: for I have espoused you to one husband, that I may present you as a chaste virgin to Christ. But I fear, lest by any means, as the serpent beguiled Eve through his subtlety, so your minds should be corrupted from the simplicity that is in Christ.*
>
> (2 Corinthians 11:2–3)

Satan is recognized as the Serpent who is still busy at his old tricky trade. Satan has such a dexterous and successful hand at deception that Paul was uneasy. Lack of simplicity could be fatal to the purity and faith of the Corinthians, just as the taste of the forbidden fruit was fatal to Eve. It was the loss of a little thing, but, with it, all was lost.

The Importance of Discipline

Finally, an undisciplined body readily exposes us to Satan's assaults. Even natural, innocent appetites and passions have to be held in with bit and bridle. Paul was aware of this: *"But I keep under my body, and bring it into subjection: lest that by any means, when I have preached to others, I myself should be a castaway"* (1 Corinthians 9:27). An undisciplined body could hurl Paul from the office of an apostle down to the fearful abyss of apostasy.

Two statements are made in reference to his body: *"keep under"* and *"bring it into subjection."* The first phrase refers to a blow to the face under the eyes. If something is restrained and suppressed by heavy blows, its power is broken. The second statement, *"bring it into subjection,"* means "to make a slave of, to treat with severity, to subject to stern and rigid discipline." The apostle saw the body as an important factor in the contest for heaven. He teaches us that if it is untrained, without the strong repressing hand of discipline, it becomes an easy prey to the assaults of Satan.

Peter gave the same directions:

> *Be sober, be vigilant; because your adversary the devil, as a roaring lion, walketh about, seeking whom he may devour: whom resist stedfast in the faith, knowing that the same afflictions are accomplished in your brethren that are in the world.*
>
> (1 Peter 5:8–9)

A listless, drowsy, sleepy, stupid state can put us under Satan's power without a struggle or even the decency of a surrender.

Remember the strong injunction of Christ to the drowsy and fainting disciples: *"Watch and pray, that ye enter not into temptation: the spirit indeed is willing, but the flesh is weak"* (Matthew 26:41).

14

Where Does Satan Attack?

This is a true saying, If a man desire the office of
a bishop, he desireth a good work. A bishop then
must be blameless, the husband of one wife,
vigilant, sober, of good behaviour, given to
hospitality, apt to teach; not given to wine, no
striker, not greedy of filthy lucre; but patient, not
a brawler, not covetous; one that ruleth well,...not
a novice, lest being lifted up with pride he fall into
the condemnation of the devil. Moreover he must
have a good report of them which are without;
lest he fall into reproach and the
snare of the devil.
—1 Timothy 3:1–4, 6–7

We have two statements in 1 Timothy regarding the appointing of men to active
and official leadership in the church. The
first statement is against appointing novices to such
leadership. *"Not a novice, lest being lifted up with pride
he fall into the condemnation of the devil."*

To put immature believers in places of spiritual
leadership causes them to become filled with pride. If

121

the young convert is put into a highly visible position, he readily falls into the same condemnation into which the Devil fell because of pride. This text from 1 Timothy gives credence to the church's almost universally accepted opinion: the Devil fell through pride.

New converts must be matured by discipline before they are put to the front. Staying behind is often a greater cross, as well as a greater virtue, than pushing or being pushed to the front. The forefront is always an unsafe place for faith until faith has grown and matured.

Men of questionable reputation who are placed in church leadership or official positions bring reproach and help the Devil in his disgraceful business. *"Moreover he must have a good report of them which are without; lest he fall into reproach and the snare of the devil."* Having men of good character and spotless reputation in the leadership of church affairs closes Satan's mouth, cuts off his revenue, and slows down his business.

We must not violate these two rules of church government by putting novices and men whose reputations are not spotless into positions of leadership. It puts the novices in an uncomfortable position, and it increases the dangerous influence of leaders who have questionable reputations. The entire church is also put in an exposed condition, endangering the whole army.

Leaders are standard-bearers whose lives are clearly visible to everyone in the church. For this reason, they should be conspicuous in spotless piety. They should be mature in age; and sound and advanced in faith, love, and sobriety.

Where Does Satan Attack?

Gifted, wise, serious, and blameless leaders will make the church strong and victorious in the day of battle. Novices in positions of church leadership create conditions that cause them to be exposed to Satan's attacks. New converts should be sheltered and trained before they are given any responsibility in the local church.

The Devil's Workshop

Young widowhood can also be a vulnerable condition for a believer in the church. Satan is always watching for any opportunity to invade the vulnerable position of the grieving widow. Paul knew the hidden traps that Satan often uses. He wrote tenderly, honestly, and with discrimination,

> *Honour widows that are widows indeed. But if any widow have children or nephews, let them learn first to show piety at home, and to requite their parents: for that is good and acceptable before God. Now she that is a widow indeed, and desolate, trusteth in God, and continueth in supplications and prayers night and day. But she that liveth in pleasure is dead while she liveth....But the younger widows refuse: for when they have begun to wax wanton against Christ, they will marry; having damnation, because they have cast off their first faith. And withal they learn to be idle, wandering about from house to house; and not only idle, but tattlers also and busybodies, speaking things which they ought not. I will therefore that the younger women marry, bear children, guide the house, give none occasion to the adversary to speak reproachfully. For some are already turned aside after Satan.*
>
> (1 Timothy 5:3–6; 11–15)

This advice helps relieve the sorrow of the young woman and puts her where her heart and hands are full of sweet and sacred responsibilities. Her time and heart are full of profitable activity. Satan has a hard job working on a person who is filled in heart and hands with the holy tasks of raising the home, state, and church of the future.

The Problem of Lust

There are strong natural desires in man that the Scriptures term *lust*. They are called the *"lusts of the flesh"* (2 Peter 2:18; see 1 John 2:16), the *"lust of the eyes"* (1 John 2:16), *"worldly lusts"* (Titus 2:12), and the *"lusts of men"* (1 Peter 4:2). These are the cravings of the senses for which the heart naturally clamors.

These lusts form the basis of inner temptation. A cunning and powerful seducer may tempt and lead an innocent person astray even when that person is not normally tempted by such allurements, but inner lusts and desires generally form the basis and provide the groundwork for Satan's insidious temptations.

James described the whole process:

> Let no man say when he is tempted, I am tempted of God: for God cannot be tempted with evil, neither tempteth he any man: but every man is tempted, when he is drawn away of his own lust, and enticed. Then when lust hath conceived, it bringeth forth sin: and sin, when it is finished, bringeth forth death.
>
> (James 1:13–15)

The term *"drawn away"* means "to lure forth." The metaphor is from hunting or fishing. As game is lured

from the forests, so man by lust is allured from the
safety of self-restraint to sin. The word *"enticed"*
means "to catch with bait."

The Scriptures demand that these lusts or desires
be banned and denounced. We can see how Satan and
the world are behind these lusts. The Gospel is a
training school in which these lusts are to be denied.

> *For the grace of God that bringeth salvation hath
> appeared to all men, teaching us that, denying un-
> godliness and worldly lusts, we should live soberly,
> righteously, and godly, in this present world.*
> (Titus 2:11–12)

This solemn declaration from Titus is made without qualification or deception. It is a declarative
statement carrying the force of an imperative demand
and also that of a condition: *"And they that are Christ's
have crucified the flesh with the affections and lusts"* (Galatians 5:24).

The work of Christ is presented as a pattern for
us to copy in destroying these lusts:

> *Forasmuch then as Christ hath suffered for us in the
> flesh, arm yourselves likewise with the same mind:
> for he that hath suffered in the flesh hath ceased from
> sin; that he no longer should live the rest of his time
> in the flesh to the lusts of men, but to the will of
> God.*
> (1 Peter 4:1–2)

We are taught that these lusts are put in opposition to the will of God. We cannot yield to them and
remain in obedience to God. No man can serve these
two masters. These lusts are the foundations and

sources of corruption. They war against the soul. We are to

> *put off concerning the former conversation the old man, which is corrupt according to the deceitful lusts; and be renewed in the spirit of your mind; and that ye put on the new man, which after God is created in righteousness and true holiness.*
>
> (Ephesians 4:22–24)

A Weakened Position

The war with Satan is concerned with these lusts. This lusting after the pleasures of the senses is not completely destroyed when we are converted to Christ. It is broken in power and weakened, but the remains, the roots, are still there. Like a tree in life, cut down at its stump, it sends up many shoots. If we allow these shoots to remain, they will help Satan in his work.

Those who are content to leave the remains of these lusts inside them will be hampered by an internal struggle. To allow sin or the tendency to sin to remain in us is fatal. It is as fatal as leaving the original natives in the land of Canaan was to the piety, peace, and prosperity of Israel. God's command to Israel was that those nations were to be destroyed completely so as to leave neither root nor branch. Israel's failure to do this was the source of untold evil for them.

Any remaining lusts are exposed conditions just as the remains of a decayed tooth are the exposed conditions of a toothache. So we are challenged, *"For if ye live after the flesh, ye shall die: but if ye through the*

Spirit do mortify the deeds of the body, ye shall live" (Romans 8:13).

In another text, we have these words: *"They that are Christ's have crucified the flesh with the affections and lusts"* (Galatians 5:24). *"Lust"* is the larger word in Scripture, including the whole world of active lusts and desires. The *"affections"* are not so much the soul's disease in its more active operations, but the diseased conditions out of which these spring.

The lusts spring from the passions and are nourished by them. They deserve the same punishment as the flesh. All of these — the flesh, the lusts, and the affections — are crucified. This puts the Christian in the best fortified condition to resist the attacks of the Devil. If these lusts remain, he is only half armed and wholly exposed.

Lack of Spiritual Growth

Low aims in the spiritual life and satisfaction with present circumstances also create an exposed condition. The Devil may visit the highlands and mountain ranges of spiritual elevation, but he makes his home in the lowlands. He will attack the strongest, most mature giant of piety, but he works his havoc and gains his spoils where the Christian slumbers in the cradle of spiritual babyhood. There is safety only in high aims, strenuous effort, and constant advance.

It is on the field of low aims and satisfied results that the Devil wins his chief victories. Spiritual growth, along with constant and sure spiritual development, are the surest safeguards against Satan's assaults and surprises. Constant growth keeps our eyes open and our hearts strong. Satan never finds growth asleep, drowsy, or weak. Onward and upward is the great battle cry. Constant advance is the steel armor in the fight with the Devil. Israel lost Canaan by not possessing Canaan. Satan has the vantage ground when we do not maintain an aggressive forward march.

When the Bible sounded the clarion call, *"Let us go on unto perfection"* (Hebrews 6:1), it was seeking to arouse the church. The believers to whom the book of Hebrews was addressed had lost the vigor and fighting ability of Christian character by feeding on milk and indulging in the lazy luxury of being children. The Scriptures raised a standard and set a goal for them to attain. The goal line was far ahead, but it was a real point, as real as the point at which their steps were delayed. They were called out of the cradle and away from the nursery to the strength, conflict, and perfection of royal maturity.

A great writer said of Wesley that he was "the first of theological statesmen." This is no great compliment. But the spiritual perception of Wesley as a man of open, divine vision is his highest eulogy. This is evidenced by the fact that he reechoed the trumpet call of the Bible and sounded it on every key and in every refrain. He sought to stir the church into forward movement and to quicken its members to seek an advanced position. The yearning for spiritual growth had diminished in their experience and had been left out of their hopes and creeds.

God gives the beginnings of faith, and these beginnings are glorious. But for us to be content with the beginnings of faith is to forfeit its possibilities and leave us open and naked to Satan. Then we become a prey to his schemes.

Where Does Satan Attack?

Making additions to our spiritual treasury is the essential condition for stability in the Christian life. Retaining and maintaining this stability gives great victory over the Devil. To stand still in our faith is to lose it. To set up camp at the place of salvation is to forfeit regenerating grace. To stop at any station of progress is to go backward. The weakness of most people is their lack of determination to stick to their objective. We are willing to pay the personal cost for great temporal success, but the price for spiritual success is often too dear for us.

Baby Christians

The tendency in religion is to be satisfied with spiritual birth and then to die in infancy. The teething phase is a perilous time for spiritual babes. The great sin of the Israelites was hugging the shores and not going up to possess the land. The marvelous glory of their entrance into Canaan was diminished by the lethargy and timidity of their advance.

Stopping and standing still in a non-growing, non-fighting condition is a position fully exposed to Satan. Many run well and fight well, but at some point their running and fighting cease. When this happens, spiritual development is arrested, and the Devil moves at once to an easy victory.

This spiritual arrest may happen during the initial steps or stages of spiritual life. The excitement and triumphs of the first stages may arrest advance and cause a standstill. This may happen before the cradle is out of sight and while the first steps of the Christian toddler are still unsteady.

It is true that Paul called the Corinthian saints *"babes in Christ"* (1 Corinthians 3:1). But this was at the point where their saintship had turned back to carnality and lost its sanctity and strength. Their great sin and backslidings were found in their babyhood — not that they began as babes, but that they stayed babes. Baby Christianity is the popular Christianity of these days. To begin as babes is expected, but to remain babes for forty years is a fearful deformity.

Spiritual stagnation sometimes happens to those in the high echelons of spiritual prominence. It is true that a few of those who have received a great spiritual baptism after conversion have crystallized around this later point of advance. However, a far greater number of preachers and other believers have crystallized around the initial experience of salvation. There may be some specimens of Christian mummies who approached maturity, but the number who were petrified in the dwarfed and cradled state is countless.

Spiritual Stagnation

However, spiritual stagnation is not confined to the initial steps. Spiritual development's lifeblood may chill and its step halt at the point of highest advance. Many Christians are so enthusiastic over some marked advance, or some higher elevation gained, that they become enchanted with the beautiful and lofty regions. They are lulled to sleep and, like Bunyan's Pilgrim, lose their enthusiasm and are unconscious of their loss. Instead of pressing on with tireless steps, they cover the future with their imaginations. Then, while their minds are filled with fantasies of their advanced positions, they do not realize that their feet have slipped backward, and that they are in the valley again. They are so happy that it is almost impossible to bring them to their senses.

It is difficult to make them understand that there are many weary and toilsome steps between their Red Sea deliverance and the Promised Land. Even after the desert has been crossed, the Jordon has been divided, and their feet have touched the sanctified soil of Canaan, there are many battles to be fought. There are enemies to be destroyed before the good land is all possessed.

It is good to have singing and shouting sanctification. But if it is not joined by marching and fighting faith, it will sing and shout itself as thin as a ghost and as dry as a desert. *"Forgetting those things which are behind, and reaching forth unto those things which are before"* (Philippians 3:13). This is the divine process by which we hold onto what we have by getting more.

Paul's marvelous career was simple, not complex. He summed it up as fighting, running, watching—the three elements of continuous advance. Many great battles have been lost by the demoralizing effects of a halt caused by a partial victory in the earlier part of the conflict. It is not easy to keep in place and march in rank when the spoils of a half-gained victory cover the ground. There is no position this side of heaven that is free from the dangers of spiritual arrest and secure from the Devil's attacks. The conflict and vigilance of advance must mark every step until our feet are within the pearly gates.

Arrested spiritual development, either in the initial or the more advanced stages, is always an exposed position. Spiritual immaturity always leaves us vulnerable to Satan's attacks.

15

Using Our Defenses

And unto the angel of the church in Sardis write;
These things saith he that hath the seven Spirits
of God, and the seven stars; I know thy works,
that thou hast a name that thou livest, and art
dead. Be watchful, and strengthen the things
which remain, that are ready to die: for I have not
found thy works perfect before God. Remember
therefore how thou hast received and heard, and
hold fast, and repent. If therefore thou shalt not
watch, I will come on thee as a thief, and thou
shalt not know what hour I will come upon thee.
Thou hast a few names even in Sardis which have
not defiled their garments; and they shall walk
with me in white: for they are worthy. He that
overcometh, the same shall be clothed in white
raiment; and I will not blot out his name out of
the book of life, but I will confess his name before
my Father, and before his angels.
—Revelation 3:1–5

L eave no room for the Devil. Be too busy for him.
Have no time and no place for him. Vacant
places invite him. The Devil loves a vacuum. A
very busy person himself, he does his biggest business
with those who have no business.

The apostle Paul, writing to the Ephesians, gave this direction: *"Neither give place to the devil"* (Ephesians 4:27). Leave no opening, no space for him. Keep him out by prepossession. Keep him out—nose, head, and all. Give him an inch, and he will take a mile.

"Give no place to the Devil." The apostle was writing about how anger can cause us to give full scope to the Devil. He comes into power and has full sway when we relinquish ourselves to the indulgence and continuance of evil passions. Our evil passions are the regions where Satan finds his favorite field and largest sphere of operation. Suppress evil and every tendency to indignation, bitterness, and wrath. Suppress and purge out every heated impulse, every unholy desire, every feeling that is not of God. The Devil's work is futile when gentleness and forgiveness reign in our spirits.

"Resist the devil, and he will flee from you" (James 4:7). This is James's curt directory for getting rid of the Devil. *"Resist"* means "to set one's self against, to withstand." Yield nothing to Satan at any point, but oppose him at every point. Always be against him, belonging to the party of the opposition as far as his plans, suggestions, and ways are concerned.

If we bravely and strongly resist what the Devil proposes, the victory is half won. To hesitate is to lose. To talk it over is to yield; to give an inch is to surrender the whole ground. The Devil cannot stand firmness, decision, and opposition. He is easily defeated if we are determined and uncompromising. Loyalty to God is ruin to Satan.

How to Resist the Devil

We are taught this same simple, important lesson in Peter, along with an addition:

Using Our Defenses

Be sober, be vigilant; because your adversary the devil, as a roaring lion, walketh about, seeking whom he may devour: whom resist stedfast in the faith, knowing that the same afflictions are accomplished in your brethren that are in the world.

(1 Peter 5:8–9)

The first part of this direction refers to the elements of personal character. What we are is of prime consideration in this conflict with the Devil. Strong, good character is fully armed. Character is revealed in all our relationships, duties, and trials. But nowhere is character more telling than in our encounters with Satan.

We must be sober, calm, and collected—free from passion or intemperance. We must always be aware of spiritual dangers and deceptions. If we are vigilant, cautious, and active, we will never be surprised or overcome because of inattention or laziness. We must remain awake because of the full apprehension of the presence of a powerful, dangerous, and cruel Foe. This is our strong defense.

As mentioned earlier, no sorrow is so pathetic as the sorrow of young widowhood. It is a sorrow exposed to Satan's attacks. Paul's direction puts widows on the defensive and guards them against the insidious attacks of the Enemy. *"I will therefore that the younger women marry, bear children, guide the house, give none occasion to the adversary to speak reproachfully. For some are already turned aside after Satan"* (1 Timothy 5:14–15). No defense is more secure against Satan than a life crowned and crowded with unselfish duties. When they are faithfully done, the Devil has no opportunity to speak reproachfully.

James directs us to *"resist"* (James 4:7) — to set ourselves against the Devil with will and thought, conscience and heart. We must hold the Word of God strictly, strongly, and rigidly. The truth of God inflexibly held will make one invincible to the Devil, unyielding to his assaults. Temptation, toil, and affliction have been put upon God's saints in all ages. But it is by this warfare with the Devil that we are perfected, established, strengthened, and settled.

"Be sober" (1 Peter 5:8), said the apostle, for your adversary, the Devil, walks about. This calm, self-collected condition, free from passion, and with the full mastery of all our powers, is essential to successful resistance of Satan. A passionate man is a weak man. A cool head and a calm heart are the conditions of successful warfare with the Devil. The apostle added the condition of vigilance: *"Be vigilant"* (v. 8), he said. Watch, give strict attention, be cautious, be active. Vigilance awakens and sobriety arouses, giving us maximum strength.

The apostle James, in his frank, practical way, said, *"Resist the devil, and he will flee from you"* (James 4:7). *"Resist"* means to set yourself against and make no concession to the Enemy. We must meet the Devil only to fight him, and we must talk with him only to withstand him. *"Whom resist,"* said Peter, *"stedfast in the faith"* (1 Peter 5:9). That is, be solid, firm, rigid in the faith. Be fixed in your beliefs, because the liberal person has no Devil — only a very friendly one, and it does not fight against him.

The Supreme Defense

If the spirit of forgiveness is always maintained and constantly exercised, it is a supreme defense against the attacks of Satan. An unforgiving spirit is not only Satan's widest door into our hearts, but also his strongest invitation and warmest welcome.

Paul urged a spirit of forgiveness as a barrier against the Devil's entrance into our lives. Paul also hastened to close the door to him by his own readiness to forgive even in advance.

> To whom ye forgive any thing, I forgive also: for if I forgave any thing, to whom I forgave it, for your sakes forgave I it in the person of Christ; lest Satan should get an advantage of us: for we are not ignorant of his devices. (2 Corinthians 2:10–11)

A spirit of forgiveness that is free from all bitterness, revenge, or retaliation has freed itself from the conditions that invite Satan, and has effectually barred his entrance. The quickest way to keep Satan out is to keep the spirit of forgiveness in. The Devil is never deeper in hell nor farther removed from us than when we can pray, *"Father, forgive them; for they know not what they do"* (Luke 23:34).

The Devil's work is much helped or much hindered by the spirit of the servants of Christ. Gentleness is becoming to the servants of Christ not only as a beautiful adorning but also as the foundation stone. Meekness and gentleness win men, for they imitate Christ's character. Rudeness, impatience, and contention are not good recruiting officers for Christ.

> And the servant of the Lord must not strive; but be gentle unto all men, apt to teach, patient, in meekness instructing those that oppose themselves; if God

*peradventure will give them repentance to the ac-
knowledging of the truth; and that they may recover
themselves out of the snare of the devil, who are
taken captive by him at his will.*

(2 Timothy 2:24–26)

Your Chief Weapon

The Devil is to be overcome. He is not only a
hypocrite, full of quiet, slippery, and artful ways, but
he is also a man of war. He is a renowned warrior of
many campaigns and many battlefields. His boldness
and skill were tested in heaven. Angels were his enemies when heaven was the scene of his conflict and
his defeat. Yet he still fights. It takes strong young
blood with fire and valor to meet him and conquer.

The Devil must be defeated. Victory over him is
victory all along the line. It takes strength and courage
to overcome him. He is no coward, no disheartened
enemy. The zeal and strength of mature faith is absolutely necessary in this battle.

The Word of God is the conquering sword in this
warfare. The believer who has his quiver full of divine
arrows is swift, strong, penetrating, and deadly to
Satan and to sin. He will be more than a conqueror
(Romans 8:37) over the Devil. The weapon used by
the Son of God in His conflict with Satan was the
Word of God, and by it, He conquered.

*"I have written unto you, young men, because ye are
strong, and the word of God abideth in you, and ye have
overcome the wicked one"* (1 John 2:14). John, the apostle
of love who was nearest the heart of his Lord, was full
of this victory. John's love was too genuine to shrink
itself into sickly sentiment or evaporate the Devil into

a mere influence. His experience was too profound and his memory too fresh to believe in an impersonal Devil or an impersonal Christ. John carried the scars of the battles with the adversary of his soul. He had witnessed the conflicts of many young soldiers. His soul had shared in their triumph and recorded their victories.

Fight the Devil and overcome him. This is John's method of becoming *"fathers"* (vv. 13–14) in spiritual power, rooted, grounded, and perfected. According to John, overcoming the Devil is prerequisite to overcoming the world.

The Safest Place

The mighty new-birth experience makes a man watchful like a sentinel at his post. When the Enemy in power is massed in the front, the believer is like a watchman. He stands on the walls of the beleaguered city like a guard over a royal prisoner. This keeping and guarding himself is safety against Satan's inflaming touch.

The faithful, vigilant Christian keeps himself pure, and Satan comes and finds nothing in him. (See John 14:30.) Every vantage point is barred and sleeplessly watched.

> We know that whosoever is born of God sinneth not; but he that is begotten of God keepeth himself, and that wicked one toucheth him not. And we know that we are of God, and the whole world lieth in wickedness ["the evil one," RV].   (1 John 5:18–19)

"Keeping ourselves" is the surest pledge that Satan will not keep us.

"Watch" is the keynote of safety. The Devil works on us with a thousand instruments, comes to us in a thousand ways, administers a thousand rebukes, and assaults by a thousand surprises. Watchfulness at all times is our only safety. We must not remain wide awake only when we see his form and fear his presence, but we must also remain wide awake to see him when he is not to be seen. We must repel him when he comes with any one of his ten thousand disguises — this is our wisest and safest course.

No cry of alarm is so frequent in the New Testament as the call to watch. No call hurts Satan so vitally or defeats him so readily as the call to watch. Being on the watchtower prevents all surprises and is essential to victory at all times.

The Son of God makes this call the keynote in many of His teachings. It is a call to be sleepless, to be vigilant, to be always ready. It is an image drawn from shepherds. In Jacob's indignant defense and protest against Laban, we see the image of the watchful shepherd: *"In the day the drought consumed me, and the frost by night; and my sleep departed from mine eyes"* (Genesis 31:40).

To watch is to be opposed to all listlessness. It implies a wakeful state as if in the presence of some great danger. It is a cautious state untouched by any slumbering influence. Drowsiness and bewilderment are gone. It quickens us against laziness and spiritual sloth.

Read how the church at Sardis was called to the exercise of watchfulness. She was put to sleep by the dulling effects of a fancy church exterior and a proper religious structure. (See Revelation 3:1–6.) The Ephesian church was advised to combine watching with persevering prayer (Ephesians 6:18). The Corinthian church was urged to watch and stand fast (1 Corinthians 16:13). The Colossians were exhorted to *"continue in prayer, and watch in the same"* (Colossians 4:2). The Thessalonians were to *"watch and be sober"* (1 Thessalonians 5:6).

Timothy, the young preacher, was to *"watch...in all things"* (2 Timothy 4:5). Peter's call was, *"Be ye therefore sober, and watch unto prayer,"* because the solemn end of all things is quickly approaching (1 Peter 4:7). Again he said, *"Be sober, be vigilant; because your adversary the devil, as a roaring lion, walketh about, seeking whom he might devour"* (1 Peter 5:8).

In Revelation we have the startling call, *"Behold, I come as a thief. Blessed is he that watcheth, and keepeth his garments, lest he walk naked, and they see his shame"* (Revelation 16:15).

The most frequent call to watchfulness was from our Lord. He said, *"Watch, therefore; for ye know not what hour your Lord doth come"* (Matthew 24:42). Again He called us to exercise this great grace: *"Watch therefore, for ye know neither the day nor the hour wherein the Son of man cometh"* (Matthew 25:13). Repeatedly, He calls us to *"watch ye therefore"* (Mark 13:35).

The herald cry and the trumpet call from Him to us is to be awake—to be fully awake, to be tremendously awake.

"Watch ye therefore, and pray always, that ye may be accounted worthy to escape all these things that shall come to pass, and to stand before the Son of man" (Luke 21:36). *"Watch and pray"* (Matthew 26:41), He charged His disciples, and so He charges us to *"watch and pray, that ye enter not into temptation: the spirit indeed is willing,*

but the flesh is weak" (v. 41). Still the flesh is weak, and watchfulness must always be united with prayer while we are in the flesh.

Satan's Greatest Fear

The martyrs who are faithful unto death, who love not their lives unto death, are victors in this warfare with the Devil:

> *And I heard a loud voice saying in heaven, Now is come salvation, and strength, and the kingdom of our God, and the power of his Christ: for the accuser of our brethren is cast down, which accused them before our God day and night. And they overcame him by the blood of the Lamb, and by the word of their testimony; and they loved not their lives unto the death.* (Revelation 12:10–11)

"The blood of the everlasting covenant" (Hebrews 13:20) must be sprinkled on the warriors who are victors against Satan. They must have a clear, conscious experience of the saving power of that blood. They must have the ability to be martyrs and witness before any company at any cost. Their characteristics mark their devotion to Christ and their experience of His salvation. *"[He] is mine, and I am his"* (Song of Solomon 2:16).

Satan cannot stand against a display of the blood of Christ. He turns pale at every view of Calvary. The flowing wounds are the signals of Satan's retreat. A heart sprinkled with the blood is holy ground on which he dares not tread. Satan trembles and cowers in the presence of the blood-sprinkled warrior.

Using Our Defenses

Satan fears the power of that blood more than the attack of a legion of archangels. The blood is like the charge of an irresistible military force that destroys everything in its path. It is the blood applied and the testimony of its application that Satan fears. The martyr who is a witness of the power of that blood is more a barrier against Satan than a wall of fire. An experience of the atoning blood is heaven's infallible protection against Satan. Those in heaven overcame the Devil in this way. We also overcome him by the blood of the Lamb and the word of our testimony.

16

Weapons That Work

Finally, my brethren, be strong in the Lord, and in the power of his might. Put on the whole armour of God, that ye may be able to stand against the wiles of the devil. For we wrestle not against flesh and blood, but against principalities, against powers, against the rulers of the darkness of this world, against spiritual wickedness in high places. Wherefore take unto you the whole armour of God, that ye may be able to withstand in the evil day, and having done all, to stand. Stand therefore, having your loins girt about with truth, and having on the breastplate of righteousness; and your feet shod with the preparation of the gospel of peace; above all, taking the shield of faith, wherewith ye shall be able to quench all the fiery darts of the wicked. And take the helmet of salvation, and the sword of the Spirit, which is the word of God: praying always with all prayer and supplication in the Spirit, and watching thereunto with all perseverance and supplication for all saints.
—Ephesians 6:10–18

Many prayers have missed the mark and been in vain because they were not combined with careful vigilance. There are many sad failures in the Christian life because watchfulness failed. The Devil's easiest target is a sleepy Christian. Many Christians have lost their souls because they failed to stay alert to Satan's attacks. Eternal vigilance is the price of political liberty. No less a price must be paid for our spiritual safety. The foolish virgins missed heaven because they failed in this virtue. Watchfulness would have brought them, along with the Bridegroom, into the high joys of heaven's most celebrated hour. (See Matthew 25:1–13.)

In the sixth chapter of Ephesians, as stated above, all the weapons of warfare with the Devil and his legions are described. The sources of defense and victory are also given. In this passage, we have a view of the strenuous conflict and the battlefield on which the issues of eternity are tossed.

Satan's Army

"For we wrestle not against flesh and blood, but against principalities, against powers, against the rulers of the darkness of this world, against spiritual wickedness in high places." The Christian's battle is with the Devil and his methods. Satan's struggle is arranged with order, wisdom, and skill.

Principalities and powers are under his management and subject to his orders. They are his lieutenants, his prime ministers, his captain generals who carry out his orders and represent him fully. They are the world rulers with worldwide control and power.

They master and control all the evil forces of the world. The Devil and his high comrades are world rulers. Their might is as extensive as the world. Theirs is a fearful rule for evil, against the good and against man. Their subordinates, the rank and file, are innumerable and invincible, except to a God-equipped man.

What a vast and powerful array of aggressive, vicious, and cruel enemies. They are in heavenly places, the very place where Christ's power is located. These evil powers are over us, above us, and around us. They are too mighty for us. Against this invisible, innumerable, all-powerful, and vast array, we wrestle. Wrestling is a close conflict. It is an intense and difficult conflict that tests all strength and strains every fiber. It is hand-to-hand, foot-to-foot, close contact.

This conflict is not with men, though men may give us much opposition in our Christian course. Our chief trouble and our great war is not with man but with all the mighty evil forces of the Devil. It is a life-and-death struggle—a war for heaven and hell, for time and eternity.

The Christian Soldier

The Christian must be a soldier by birth, by fortune, by trade. The most essential quality of a divine soldier is that he is not entangled *"with the affairs of this life"* (2 Timothy 2:4). The elements of self-denial, courage, and endurance are the vital characteristics of this military training.

Strength is the fruit of these high qualities. But it is strength far beyond the Christian soldier's own strength. *"Strong in the Lord, and in the power of his might"* (Ephesians 6:10). In preparation for this war, the soldier must look beyond himself. The strength of God, the very strength of God's almightiness, must be his.

The ability to stand, to fight, to conquer, and to drive the Foe from the field will be found in God's armor. God's strength is imparted through God's armor. No power short of God can enable us to meet the Devil. No partial equipment will suffice.

In the passage from Ephesians, we are charged twice to make doubly sure to take the whole armor (Ephesians 6:11, 13). We take God by taking His armor. We must make His armor our own. We put on God by putting on His armor—not outside but inside, not objective but subjective, not physical but spiritual. Christ made the armor, and the Holy Spirit puts it on us and makes it ours.

We have to fight through to the end, *"and having done all, to stand."* We must first withstand and then stand. We gain and hold and then advance. Stand ready for the fight and stand in the fight.

Truth and Righteousness

We must be strong for the *"truth in the inward parts"* (Psalm 51:6). We are not imaginary soldiers fighting an imaginary war—all is real and true. Because he is truthful, a girded soldier is strong, prepared, and intense in his fight. Truth is the ornament of a jeweled belt, a diamond set in gold. We must conquer the Devil by truth as the strength and support of our lives. We know the truth and have the truth because we have Christ who is the truth.

Weapons That Work

Heart righteousness makes head righteousness and life righteousness. We cannot fight without heart righteousness. The *"breastplate of righteousness"* protects the heart and makes us feel right. The old heart cannot be made right by the most skillful craftsman or by the most correct rituals. No tinkering on the old heart can make it right. It is as hard as a stone and as crooked as the Jordan. No melting can make it soft, and no human effort can make it straight. We need a new heart, soft as flesh and washed whiter than snow in the blood of Christ. A piece of Christ's heart—perfect, right, pure, and good—is what is needed.

Preparation and Faith

The feet must be shod with a preparation that is always ready to go, to do, and to suffer. This means no slow movements or reluctant doing of God's will. Being off guard creates a general unreadiness for life or death, for earth or heaven, for sacrifice or service, for doing or for suffering. It cuts the nerve of Christian valor and lays us open to surprises and crushing defeats. "Always ready" is the soldier's attitude of safety, and being ready to move precedes victory. Wakeful vigilance assures us of victory against the Devil.

The *"shield of faith"* is the all-important and all-covering piece of armor. The Devil lets his fiery, poisoned darts fly, but faith catches them as they are directed at head or heart, and quenches them.

Do you believe all victories are possible to the soldier who is valiant and strong in faith? There has never been a battle planned by hell's most gifted strategist that can conquer faith. All his flaming and terrible darts fall harmless as they strike against the shield of faith. *"These all died in faith"* (Hebrews 11:13). Faith made their death the crowning point. Faith brought to their dying hour the spoils of their victories.

The Helmet and Sword

"The helmet" protects the head. Bear in mind that head-salvation and heart-salvation, real and full, are stronger than brass to protect the head. A heart fully saved holds the head firmly to truth and righteousness, as the anchor holds the ship in stormiest seas. *"The hope of salvation,"* said Paul in Thessalonians, is the helmet (1 Thessalonians 5:8).

The Christian soldier must put heaven strongly in his head and heart. He must see heaven, feel heaven, and keep heaven in the eye and in the heart all the time. He will stand with unsteady step if heaven seems far off. He will fight feebly if heaven is dimly seen. The full sight of heaven will give strength to his loins, zeal to his faith, glory to his future, and victory to the present.

The head will never be pierced while hope is its helmet. Nurture hope, strengthen hope, and brighten hope, for *"we are saved by hope"* (Romans 8:24). We must *"abound in hope, through the power of the Holy Ghost"* (Romans 15:13).

"The sword," the aggressive and powerful weapon, is the Word of God. The Spirit wields it and brings death to all our foes. The Word of God is our battlefield and victorious weapon. On it we stand and fight. With it we deal with and defeat and ruin every

Weapons That Work

foe. The Christian soldier is *"not* [to] *live by bread alone, but by every word...of God"* (Matthew 4:4). We cannot make too much of the Word of God. Christ foiled Satan with it. If we are to be valiant, true, and invincible, we also must have the Word of God dwelling in us richly (Colossians 3:16).

The shield of our faith is the basis of our prayers and the essence of our girded truth. Head, hands, and hearts must be filled and saturated with God's Word; by it we live and by it we grow. It is our battle call and the sign by which we conquer. It is a glittering royal blade against all the assaults of Satan. "It is written" goes like steel to the heart of Satan.

As a weapon of defense and offense, God has magnified His Word above all His name. Those who are filled with God's Word are armed against all Satan's wiles and his devices. God's Word is *"quick, and powerful, and sharper than any twoedged sword, piercing even to the dividing asunder of soul and spirit, and of the joints and marrow"* (Hebrews 4:12). Satan feels it penetrating his joints and marrow, dissolving into weakness all his strength, and making foolish all his wisest plans.

The Weapon of Prayer

The soldiers in the warfare against the Devil must understand how to wear the armor of *"all prayer."* The demand is for *"all prayer"* at all seasons, in the intensest form, with a deep sense of personal need for God. Prayer must deepen and intensify into supplication. The Holy Spirit will help us into this kind of mighty praying and clothe us with this irresistible power of prayer.

This intense conflict with the Devil requires sleepless vigilance, midnight vigils, and a wakefulness that cannot be surprised. It also requires a perseverance that knows neither halting, fainting, nor depression. This kind of praying knows by clear spiritual intelligence what it needs. The prayer warrior knows the unlimited provisions that are available to supply all his needs. He knows the necessity of perseverance in prayer until the need is supplied and the provision is secured.

This kind of praying holds itself in loving sympathy with the entire family of God, making their conflicts, dangers, and needs its own. It is on the line of battle with the whole family of God. It takes on their enemies, their safety, and their dangers. *"Supplication for all saints"* gives victory to every saint. The line of battle is one. Defeat or victory must come to all. The soldier fully equipped in God's armor is a veteran against the Devil and invincible to all of his attacks.

It is not an easy thing to pray. Behind the praying there must lie the conditions of prayer. These conditions are possible, but they cannot be achieved in a moment by the prayerless person. They are always available to the faithful and holy, but cannot exist in a frivolous, negligent, and lazy spirit.

Prayer does not stand alone. It is not an isolated performance. Prayer is connected to all the duties of the Christian life. Prayer issues from a character that is made up of the elements of a vigorous and commanding faith. Prayer honors God, acknowledges His being, exalts His power, adores His providence, and secures His aid.

A skeptic would rationalize and cry out against devotion, charging that it does nothing but pray. But to pray well is to do all things well. If it is true that devotion does nothing but pray, then it really does do nothing at all, for the conditions of prayer are the sum of *all* the energized forces and all the duties of practical working Christianity.

The Power of Prayer

Prayer brings God into the situation with commanding force. *"Ask me of things to come concerning my sons,"* says God, *"and concerning the work of my hands command ye me"* (Isaiah 45:11).

We are charged in God's Word: *"Pray without ceasing"* (1 Thessalonians 5:17). *"In every thing by prayer"* (Philippians 4:6). *"Continuing instant in prayer"* (Romans 12:12). *"Pray every where"* (1 Timothy 2:8). *"Praying always"* (Colossians 1:3).

The promise is as unlimited as the command is comprehensive. *"All things, whatsoever ye shall ask in prayer, believing, ye shall receive"* (Matthew 21:22). Jesus said, *"Whatsoever ye shall ask"* (John 14:13); *"if ye shall ask any thing"* (John 14:14); *"ye shall ask what ye will, and it shall be done unto you"* (John 15:7); and *"whatsoever ye shall ask the Father…he will give it you"* (John 16:23).

If there is anything not involved in *"all things whatsoever,"* or not found in the phrase, *"ask any thing,"* then these things can be left out of prayer. Language could not cover a wider range or involve more fully every detail of life. These statements are only samples of the all-comprehending possibilities of prayer under the promises of God to those who meet the conditions of right praying.

These passages, though, give only a general outline of the immense regions over which prayer extends its influence. The effect of prayer reaches and secures good things from regions that cannot be covered by language or thought. Paul exhausted his language and thought when he was praying. Still, he was conscious of necessities not covered, realms of good not reached, and of battles over enemies not conquered.

Paul covered these undiscovered regions by this general plea: *"Unto him that is able to do exceeding abundantly above all that we ask or think, according to the power that worketh in us"* (Ephesians 3:20). The promise is, *"Call unto me, and I will answer thee, and show thee great and mighty things, which thou knowest not"* (Jeremiah 33:3).

About the Author

Edward McKendree Bounds was born in Shelby County, Missouri, on August 15, 1835, and died on August 24, 1913, in Washington, Georgia. He received a public school education at Shelbyville and was admitted to the bar soon after he reached adulthood. He practiced law until called to preach the Gospel at the age of twenty-four.

His first pastorate was in the Monticello, Missouri, circuit. It was while he was serving as pastor in Brunswick, Missouri, that the Civil War began. The young minister was made a prisoner of war because he would not take the oath of allegiance to the federal government. He was sent to St. Louis and later transferred to Memphis, Tennessee.

Finally securing his release, Bounds traveled on foot nearly one hundred miles to join General Pierce's command in Mississippi and was soon after made chaplain of the Fifth Missouri Regiment, a position he held until near the close of the war, when he was captured and held as prisoner at Nashville, Tennessee.

After the war, Bounds was pastor of churches in Tennessee and Alabama. In 1875 he was assigned to St. Paul Methodist Church in St. Louis, where he served for four years. After filling several other pastorates, he was sent to the First Methodist Church in

St. Louis, Missouri, for one year and again to St. Paul Methodist Church for three years. At the end of his pastoral career, he became the editor of the *St. Louis Christian Advocate.*

In 1876, in Eufaula, Alabama, he married Emma Elizabeth Barnett, who died ten years later. In 1887 he married Emma's cousin, Harriet Elizabeth Barnett, who survived him. The family included five children, as well as two daughters from his first marriage.

He was a forceful writer and a very deep thinker. He spent the last seventeen years of his life with his family in Washington, Georgia. Most of the time he was reading, writing, and praying. He arose at four o'clock each morning for many years and was indefatigable in his study of the Bible. His writings were read by thousands of people and were in demand by people of every Protestant denomination.

Bounds was the embodiment of humility, with an angelic devotion to Jesus Christ. He reached that high place where self is forgotten and the love of God and humanity is the all-absorbing thought and purpose.

When he was seventy-six years of age, he came to visit me in Brooklyn, New York, and he was so intense that he awoke me and my family at three o'clock in the morning, praying and weeping over the lost of the earth. All during the day he would go into the church next door and be found on his knees until he was called for his meals. This is what he called the "business of praying."

H. W. HODGE

ANOTHER POWERFUL *Book*

from Whitaker House

ISBN: 0-88368-559-0
Trade
299 pages

God's Best Secrets
Andrew Murray

In this devotional, Andrew Murray shares the personal revelation that he gained from spending quiet time alone with God. Discover the secrets of fellowship, prayer, faith, and more as you enter into the wonderful privileges that are open to you in *God's Best Secrets*.

ANOTHER POWERFUL *B*OOK
from Whitaker House

ISBN: 0-88368-682-1
Trade
208 pages

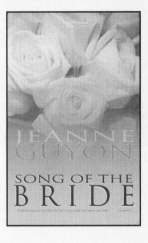

Song of the Bride
Jeanne Guyon

The greatest love story ever written, the Song of
Songs describes the emotional, unfolding story of the
Bridegroom and His bride. Jeanne Guyon shows how
the song of a young maiden, fervently in love with her
suitor, becomes a powerful allegory of every believer's
relationship with Christ. You will be drawn to God's
heart as you read this book.

ANOTHER POWERFUL BOOK

from Whitaker House

Spiritual Warfare
Derek Prince

Derek Prince explains the battle that's happening now between the forces of God and the forces of evil. Choose to be prepared by learning the enemy's strategies so you can effectively block his attack. We have God on our side and nothing will keep us from victory.

ISBN: 0-88368-670-8
Trade
144 pages